# THE
# LIGHT
## OF
# WISDOM

Kabbalah Publishing is a registered DBA of
The Kabbalah Centre International, Inc.

For further information:

The Kabbalah Centre
155 E. 48th St., New York, NY 10017
1062 S. Robertson Blvd., Los Angeles, CA 90035

1.800.Kabbalah  www.kabbalah.com

First Edition, January 2015

Printed in USA

ISBN: 978-157189-943-9

Design: HL Design (Hyun Min Lee)  www.hldesignco.com

# The
# Light
## of
# Wisdom

### On Wisdom, Life, and Eternity

KABBALAH
CENTRE
PUBLISHING

*Rav Yehuda Ashlag*

EDITED BY MICHAEL BERG

# Table of Contents

**Chapter 22: A *Tzadik* (Righteous Person) Comes to the World**

**Chapter 23: Peace is a Fitting Vessel to Contain Blessing**

## *Foreword*

It is with great joy that we are able to make this book available to the English-speaking public. It was originally written in Hebrew by the great Kabbalist and founder of The Kabbalah Centre, Rav Yehuda Ashlag, as an introduction to his commentary on Rav Isaac Luria's book entitled *Tree of Life*. The original book and commentary were the beginnings of the revelation by Rav Ashlag.

In order to receive the full benefit, Light, and revelation that this book has to offer, it would be beneficial to understand the soul and Light of Rav Yehuda Ashlag in a deeper way.

Rav Ashlag writes that there are two types of prophets: A great prophet and a lesser prophet. He explains that although both prophets receive and give over the true message, the difference is in the length of the path revealed by the prophet. As he writes, "Even though ultimately all the truth in the prophecy is revealed with the desired success, still this lesser prophet has caused the prophecy to take a longer road to the people to whom he was sent with his prophecy. This is unlike the greater prophet whose preparation is more complete, and who therefor does not experience any deviation when he receives the prophecy from the Creator. For this reason, he does not use a greater number of channels and vessels. Therefore his prophecy is clear and concise, and is easily and quickly adopted by those to whom he was sent. Suppose, for example, that his prophecy is sent to 100 people: If it is going through a long way, it can bring to completion only one person in a generation, and if so, then the duration of his prophecy will be 100 years. If he takes a shorter route, clearly he will bring 30 or 50 people to completion in a generation, and obviously his prophecy will be completed within only a few years." (*On World Peace*, page 108)

Although Rav Ashlag does not expressly write this, there is no question that these words refer to him and his revelation of the secrets to our generation. Therefore it is understandable that by studying from his words we avail ourselves of the quickest path to change and connection to the Light of the Creator. A path our generation desperately needs.

Rav Ashlag continues to explain the express purpose of prophecy, and in truth the purpose of his life and teachings: "The principle of prophetic success is the extending of the exalted Light to those dwelling below. And the prophet who is able to bring the light to the lowest level is the one who is most successful." (*On World Peace*, page 109) This is what Rav Ashlag's writing are meant to reveal, to create a path for all of humanity to easily access the Supernal Light of the Creator.

Rav Ashlag's writings are "the teachings of the Messiah," which means that they are the path for not only individual elevation and connection but ultimately the path for humanity as a whole to become elevated to completely connect and receive the Supernal Light of the Creator. At the end of this process, we achieve the state of removal of pain, suffering, and death from the world.

It is my hope that the publication of this book and its study by you, the reader, will bring each one of us individually, and the world as a whole, one step closer to the prophecy "and the world will be filled with the knowledge of the Creator as the waters cover the ocean," (*Isaiah* 11:9) and then "death will be swallowed up forever." (*Isaiah* 25:8)

Blessings,
Michael Berg

# Chapter 1: A Vessel to Contain Blessing

## Peace and Strength

(1-1) At the end of [Tractate] *Uk'tzin*, [it is said that] the Creator did not find any Vessel to contain the blessing for the Israelites other than [the Vessel of] peace, as it is said: "May the Creator give strength to His people; may the Creator bless His people with peace!" (Psalms 29:11) And one should study this deeply. First, where is the proof that there is nothing better for the Israelites than peace? Second, the Scripture explicitly says that peace is the very blessing itself, for about strength it is written: "giving," and about peace it says, "blessing." So according to this, should it not have said, "*giving* in peace"? And third, why was this saying put at the end of the *Shas* (the 'six orders' of the *Mishnah*)?

(1-2) We must also understand the meaning of the words "peace" and "strength" as well as their significance. In order to explain this saying according to its real meaning, we must go through a lengthy path. This is because the depth of the heart of the sages of the *Agadah* (*Book of Homilies*) is unfathomable. Therefore, the author of *Afikei Yehudah* was right when he said in his explanation of the words of our sages on the passage, "sustain me with silverware" (Song of Songs 2:5) that it refers to *Halachah* (Biblical rules), while "refresh me with apples" (ibid.) refers to the *Agadah*. And our sages said that in all matters of the Torah and the Precepts, there are both Revealed and Concealed layers, as it is said: "A word fitly spoken is like apples of gold in a setting of silver." (Proverbs 25:11).

## Inner and Outer

(1-3) Indeed, the *Halachah* (Biblical rules) resemble silver wine goblets. When someone gives his friend wine in a silver goblet as a gift, both what is inside and what is outside are important. This is because the goblet also has value in itself, just like the wine it

4

# פרק א: כלי של ברכה

## שלום ועוז

(א-1) בשלהי [מסכת] עוקצין [כתוב], לא מצא הקב"ה כלי מחזיק ברכה לישראל אלא השלום, שנאמר (בספר תהילים כט' יא'): ה' עוז לעמו יתן ה' יברך את עמו בשלום. ויש להשכיל בו רבות, [שאלה] א', מאין הוכיחו שאין יותר טוב לישראל מהשלום. [שאלה] ב' שבהכתוב מפורש שהשלום היא הברכה בעצמה, שכתוב נתינה בעוז וברכה בשלום ולדבריהם הי' היה לו לומר נתינה בשלום. [שאלה] ג', למה נתחבר מאמר הזה לסיום הש"ס שישה סדרי [משנה].

(א-2) גם צריך להבין פי' פירוש המלות דשלום ועוז, והורתם. וכדי לפרש מאמר הזה על תכנו האמיתי, מוכרחין אנו לבוא בדרך ארוכה. כי עומק לב בעלי הגדה לאין חקר. ובצדק דיבר הרב בעל [מחבר ספר] אפיקי יהודא ז"ל, בפי' בפירוש דברי חז"ל. על הפסוק (שיר השירים ב' ה'), 'סמכוני באשישות' אלו הלכות, 'רפדוני בתפוחים' אלו הגדות, ופי' ופירשו [חכמינו] ז"ל, כי כל ענייני התורה והמצוה, יש בהם נגלה ונסתר, כמוש, כמו שכתוב תפוחי זהב במשכיות כסף דבר דבר על אופניו (משלי כה' יא').

## חיצוניות ופנימיות

(א-3) אומנם ההלכות דומין לאשישי יין, אשר הנותן לחבירו מתנה גביע כסף עם יין, הרי תוכו וברו שניהם חשובים, שהרי גם הגביע

contains. But this is not the case with the *Agadah* (*Book of Homilies*). The *Agadah* is like an apple, the inner part of which is eaten and the outer part of which is thrown away.

(1-4) This is because the outer part has no value whatsoever, the entire value is found in the inner part and the core. And the same applies to the words of the *Agadah*, as their literal and obvious [that is, the outer] aspect has no meaning or value at all; indeed, the only valuable part is the inner content that is concealed within the words, which are based solely on the Wisdom of Truth that is mastered by [lit. given to] only the select few (end of quote [from *Afikei Yehudah*], with some changes of words).

## The PaRDeS – *Peshat, Remez, Derash, Sod*

(1-5) Who would dare to take this out of the heart of the masses and investigate their ways because their understanding is not complete even in the two aspects of the Torah referred to as *Peshat* (Literal) and *Derash* (Allegorical)? The order, according to the masses, in which the four levels of the Torah—the PaRDeS [*Peshat* (literal), *Remez* (logical inference), *Derash* (allegorical), and *Sod* (secret)]—should be studied is [that] the understanding of the *Peshat* [comes] first, then the *Derash*, then the *Remez*, and at the end everyone will understand the *Sod*.

(1-6) Yet we have found in the *siddur* (prayer book) of the Vilna Gaon, Rav Eliyahu, that the *Sod* is the level from which proper understanding starts, and [only] after these secrets of the Torah are obtained can we perceive the *Derash*. After that, we can perceive the level of the *Remez*, and only after we merit completing ourselves and mastering these three aspects of the Torah can we merit perceiving the *Peshat* aspect of the Torah (end of his words).

יש לו ערך בפני עצמו, כמו היין שבתוכו, משא"כ מה שאין כן ההגדות, המה נמשלים לתפוחים, שתוכו נאכל וחיצוניותו נזרקת.

(א-4) שאין להחיצוניות ערך של כלום, ונמצא כל הערך והחשיבות רק בהפנימיות והתוך. וכן בדברי הגדה אין בהפשטיות הנראה לעינים שום מובן וחפץ, זולת בתוכן הפנימי הגנוז בהדברים, שאינם נבנים אלא על אדני חכמת האמת, המסור ליחידי סגולה, עכ"ל עד כאן לשונו [של אפיקי יהודא] בשינוי לשון.

**פשט, רמז, דרש, סוד**

(א-5) ומי יהן להוציא זה מלב ההמון, ולברר דרכיהם, שאין השגתם שלימה גם בשני חלקי התורה הנק' הנקראים פשט ודרוש. אשר סדר ד' חלקי התורה פרד"ס פשט, רמז, דרש, סוד לפי דעתם, שמתחילה מבינים הפשט, ואח"כ ואחר כך הדרוש, ואח"כ ואחר כך הרמז, ובסוף הכל מבינים הסוד.

(א-6) אמנם איתא מובא, בסידור הגר"א הגאון רבי אליהו [מוילנא] ז"ל שתחילת ההשגה מתחלת מהסוד, ואחר שמשיגין חלק הסוד שבתורה, אפשר להשיג חלק הדרוש ואח"כ ואחר כך חלק הרמז ואחר שזוכה האדם להשתלם בג' חלקי התורה האלו על בוריים, אז זוכה להשיג חלק הפשט שבתורה ע"כ עד כאן.

## Potion of Life and Potion of Death

(1-7) And this is what our sages meant when they said in Tractate *Ta'anit* (7a): "If a person merits, it becomes a potion of life; if a person does not merit, it becomes a potion of death" (end of quote). Great merit is needed in order to understand the literal meaning of the text, since we are obligated to comprehend the three aspects of the inner [part of the] Torah that are clothed with the *Peshat* (Literal) first, otherwise, [the covers of] the *Peshat* (Literal) cannot be *yufshat* (made simpler, also unveiled).

(1-8) If a person has not yet merited this [understanding], then a great amount of mercy is required so that the Torah will not become for that person a potion of death, Heaven forbid. This is the opposite of the claims of those who are neglectful in perceiving the inner part, as they say to themselves, "We are satisfied with grasping the *Peshat*, and how we wish to be able to understand it, for then we would be happy and content." Their words are like those of someone who wants to step onto the fourth step [of the stairs] without climbing the first three steps.

## סם חיים וסם המוות

(א-7) והיינו דאמרו [חכמינו] ז"ל במסכת תענית (דף ז', עמוד א') זכה נעשה לו סם חיים לא זכה נעשה לו סם מות ע"כ עד כאן. כי לזכיה גדולה אנו צריכים להבין בפשטי המקראות. להיותינו מחוייבים להשיג מקודם ג' החלקים שבפנימיות התורה, אשר הפשט מלביש אותם, והפשט לא יופשט.

(א-8) ואם עדיין לא זכה לזה, לרחמים גדולים הוא צריך שלא יהי' יהיה נעשית לו סמא דמותא סם המות ח"ו חס ושלום, ולאפוקי ולהבדיל מטענת המתרשלים בהשגת הפנימיות, ואומרים בלבם דיינו בהשגת הפשט, והלוואי שנשיג אותה, והיינו שמחים בחלקינו, שדבריהם דומים למי שרוצה לעלות על המדרגה הרביעית, בטרם שיפסוע על ג' מדרגות הראשונות .

# Chapter 2: Temporary Concealment

## Spreading the Wisdom of Kabbalah

(2-1) Indeed, according to this, we should understand the great concealment that is customary with regard to the inner part of the Torah, as was said in Tractate *Hagigah* (11b): "One should not study the Act of Creation in [a group of] two, nor should one study [the story of] *Merkavah* (Chariot) [even] alone." And likewise, all the books that are available to us on this subject [of Kabbalah] are sealed and blocked to the eyes of the masses. They would not understand, except for those select few who are called upon by the Creator, being that they already understand the Roots on their own and by receiving [this knowledge from a teacher] Mouth to Mouth.

(2-2) There is a great wonder here as to why spreading this Wisdom [of Truth] and understanding is blocked from the people, [considering that this wisdom] is their very life and length of days. And this [denial] would seemingly be a criminal transgression, which is why our sages said in the *Midrash Rabbah* on Genesis concerning [King] Achaz that he was called Achaz [lit. to hold back or prevent] because he prevented [the building of] synagogues and spiritual schools, etc., and therefore, his guilt was great, etc.

(2-3) And it is a [universal] law of nature that one feels reluctant to confer his wealth and riches upon others, but is there anyone who feels reluctant to confer his wisdom and understanding upon others? On the contrary, "Even more than the calf wants to be fed, the cow wishes to feed," (Tractate *Pesachim,* 112) how much more so [is this the case] when it comes to the Creator's Torah and His Will.

## Without Preconditions

(2-4) Indeed, we do find mysteries in wisdom, even among the secular [lit. external] wise men of ages past. We have learned from the late Rav Moshe Butril, in the introduction to his commentary

# פרק ב: הסתרה זמנית

## הפצת חכמת הקבלה

(ב-1) אמנם לפי"ז לפי זה צריכים להבין ההעלמה הגדולה הנוהגת בפנימיות התורה, כמש"א כמו שאמרו [חז"ל] במסכת חגיגה [דף יא', עמוד ב']: אין דורשין במעשה בראשית בשנים ולא במרכבה ביחיד. וכן כל הספרים המצויים לנו במקצוע הזה, חתומים וסתומים לעיני כל ההמון לא יבינו זולת השרידים אשר ה' קורא אותם, בהיותם כבר מבינים את השרשים, מדעתם, ובקבלה מפה אל פה.

(ב-2) אשר הוא תמיה רבתי איך מונעים תהלוכות החכמה והתבונה מקרב העם אשר הוא כל חייהם ואורך ימיהם, ולכאורה הוא עון פלילי שע"כ שעל כן אמרו [חכמינו] ז"ל במדרש רבה, בראשית על אחז שע"כ שעל כן נקרא אחז בשביל שאחז בתי כנסיות ובתי מדרשות וכו', דע"כ שעל כן גדלה אשמתו וכו'.

(ב-3) וכן חוק הטבע אשר עינו של אדם צרה, להאציל מהונו ורכושו לאחרים, אבל כלום יש לך מי שעינו צרה, מלהאציל מחכמתו ותבונתו על אחרים, ואדרבה ביותר ממה שהעגל רוצה לינוק הפרה רוצה להניק (פסחים קי"ב). ומכ"ש ומכל שכן בתורת ה' וחפצו ית'.

## בלי תנאים מוקדמים

(ב-4) אמנם כן אנו מוצאים תעלומות בחכמה, אפי' בחכמים החיצונים, בדורות שעברו. ואיתא ומובא בהקדמתו של הר"מ הרב

on *Sefer Yetzirah* (*The Book of Formation*), of an article by Plato who warns his students as follows: "Do not pass on this wisdom to someone who cannot appreciate its virtues." And Aristotle warned: "Do not give out wisdom to someone who is not worthy of it, for fear that you will destroy it." Moreover, [Rav Moshe Butril] commented that if the wise man teaches wisdom to someone who is not worthy of it, he destroys the wisdom and mutilates it (end of quote).

(2-5) This is not what the secular wise men are doing in our times. On the contrary, they are making an effort to widen the gates of their wisdom for all the masses [to enter] without any boundaries and conditions. And seemingly, there is a great contention [now] with those earlier men of wisdom who closed the gates of their wisdom, [allowing only] a select few and unique, whom they found fit for that [knowledge, to enter], while the majority of the people were left to grope their way in darkness.

משה בוטריל ז"ל לפירושו על ספר היצירה, מאמר בשם אפלטון שהזהיר לתלמידיו כלשון הזה "אל תמסרו החכמה למי שאינו יודע מעלתה", וכן הזהיר אריסטו "אל תמסרו החכמה למי שאין ראוי לה פן תחמסוה" והוא [רבי משה בוטריל] ז"ל פירשו, אשר אם החכם מלמד חכמה למי שאינו הגון לה, הוא חומס את החכמה ומשחיתה, עכ"ל עד כאן לשונו.

(ב-5) ולא כן עושים חכמים החיצונים שבדורותינו, אלא אדרבא מתאמצים להרחיב שערי חכמתם לכל מרחבי ההמון, בלי שום גדרים ותנאים. ולכאורה יש טענה גדולה על חכמיהם הראשונים, שסגרו דלתי חכמתם על קומץ קטן מיחידי סגולה, שמצאו מוכשרים אלי' ו[את] מרבית העם עזבו לגשש קיר.

# *Chapter 3: Varied World*

## Inanimate, Vegetative, Animal, and Speaking (Human)

(3-1) I shall explain the situation, four different classes of people can be distinguished among the Speaking species (mankind), and they are arranged hierarchically. These classes are: the masses, the heroes, the wealthy, and the wise. They are in essence equal to the four levels in the whole of reality, which are called: Inanimate, Vegetative, Animal, and Speaking (human). The Inanimate has the ability to bring out the qualities of the other three levels: Vegetative, Animal, and Speaking.

(3-2) We can distinguish [among these latter] three levels in terms of the beneficial and damaging forces contained within them. The least powerful force among the three is in the Vegetative [domain]. Although the plant, by attracting that which is useful to it and rejecting that which is harmful to it, is similar to human and animal species. It does not have any particular sense that is dedicated to doing so, rather, it has a general common force that is common to all the plants in the world, where such a function applies.

(3-3) In addition [to the Vegetative level], there is the Animal species, where each and every creature has an individual feeling of its own in terms of attracting that which is beneficial and rejecting that which is harmful. From this, we can conclude that the value of a single animal is equal to the value of all the plants in this reality. This is because the force that feels and distinguishes between that which is beneficial and that which is harmful in the entirety of the Vegetative species is contained in one individual animal that is separate unto itself. But this power of sentience that exists in the Animal species is limited by time and space because it does not relate to anything that is even marginally distant from its body. [An animal] also has no ability to sense anything beyond its own time, that is to say, [in its] past or future; it can only sense that particular moment it is in [and nothing else].

# פרק ג: עולם רב גוני

## דומם, צומח, חי, מדבר

(ג-1) ואסביר הענין, כי ד' מפלגות אנו מבחינים במין המדבר, במדרגה זה על זה, שהם: המון עם, גבורים, עשירים, חכמים, והם שוים בערך, לד' מדרגות שבכלל המציאות, הנקרא דומם צומח, חי, מדבר. אשר הדומם, מוכשר להוציא ג' הסגולות, צומח, חי, מדבר.

(ג-2) ואנו מבחינים ג' ערכים, בכמות הכח מהמועיל והמזיק שיש בהם. כח הקטן שבהם, הוא הצומח, כי הגם שפעולת הצמח, בקרבת המועיל שלה ובדחית המזיק לה דומה, למין האדם והחי, אמנם אין בה הרגש נבדל לענין זה אלא כח כללי משותף לכל מיני הצמחים שבעולם, שפועל בהם מלאכה הזו.

(ג-3) נוסף עליהם מין החי, שבכל ברי' בריה וברי' ובריה בפני עצמה יש הרגש פרטי לעצמו, לקרבת המועיל ולהרחקת המזיק, ויוצא לנו בזה, ערך בעל חי פרטי אחד, משתוה עם ערך כל מיני הצמחים שבהמציאות כי זה כח המרגיש בברורי מועיל ומזיק, שישנם לכללות כל מין הצומח, נמצא בברי' בריה פרטית אחת ממין החי נבדל ברשותו לעצמו. והנה כח המרגיש הזה הנוהג במין החי, הוא מוגבל מאוד במקום ובזמן, להיות ההרגש אינו פועל בריחוק מקום כחוט השערה מחוץ לגופו, וכו' אינו מרגיש מחוץ לזמנו, כלומר, בעבר ובעתיד, אלא באותו רגע שהוא דבוק בה לבד.

*Human*

(3-4) And to these, the species of the Speaking is added. [This species] possesses the power of sentience and the power of reasoning together, and therefore, its power is not limited by time and space, [enabling a human] to attract that which is beneficial and reject that which is harmful, like the Animal species [is limited]. This is because of its knowledge that is a spiritual essence and is not confined by time and space; [thus, the Speaking species] can learn about all created beings, wherever they may be in the whole of reality as well as for many years into the past and the future.

## The Masses, the Wealthy, the Heroes, and the Men of Wisdom

(3-5) And therefore, we find that the value of one individual of the Speaking species is equal to the value of the total powers within the Vegetative and Animal species existing in the whole of reality at the present time, as well as in all past generations. It is because his power contains [lit. surrounds] theirs, and he includes within his own individuality all of their forces put together.

(3-6) This rule also applies to the four different classes of the level of human beings, which are the masses, the wealthy, the heroes, and the men of wisdom. It is sure that all of them arise from the masses, which form the first stage, according to [the verse]: "Everything is from dust." (Ecclesiastics 3:20) Indeed, the entire value and right to exist of the dust is [derived from] the value of the three levels of the Vegetative, the Animal, and the Speaking that emerge out of it.

(3-7) So, too, can the significance of the masses be valued according to the qualities that emerge from it, therefore they, too, take part in the form of the human face. For this purpose, the Creator has instilled in the general population the three qualities [lit. tendencies] named Jealousy, Desire (Greed), and Honor (Status), through which the masses evolve, step by step, until a complete human being emerges out of them.

(ג-4) נוסף עליהם מין המדבר, המורכב מכח המרגיש וכח השכלי יחד ולפיכך אין כחו מוגבל בזמן ומקום, לקרבת המועילו ולהרחקת המזיק לו, כמו מין החי, והא בסיבת המדע שלו, שהוא ענין רוחני, שאינו מוגבל בזמן ומקום, ויכול להשכיל בכל הבריות למקומותיהם בכל המציאות, וכן בעוברות ועתידות משנות דור ודור.

### המון עם, עשירים, גיבורים, חכמים

(ג-5) ונמצא ע״כ על כן, ערך איש פרטי אחד ממין המדבר, משתוה עם ערך כללות הכחות, שבמין הצמחים ומין החי, שישנם בכל המציאות בזה הזמן, וכן בכל הדורות שעברו, להיות כחו מקיף אותם, וכולל בפרטיותו עצמו, לכל כוחותיהם יחד.

(ג-6) ומשפט הזה נוהג ג״כ גם כן בד' המפלגות שבבמדרגת מין האדם דהיינו המון עם, עשירים, גבורים, חכמים, דודאי כולם באים מן המון העם, שהם הדרגה הא', ע״ד על דרך הכל הי' היה מן העפר (קוהלת ג', כ'), ואמנם ודאי כל מעלתה, וזכות קיומה של העפר, הוא לפי ערך ג' הסגולות צ. צומח, ח. חי, מדבר, שהיא מוציאה מתוכה.

(ג-7) כן ישוער מעלת ההמון עם, כפי הסגולות שמוציאים מתוכה, דע״כ שעל כן מתחברים גם המה בצורת פני אדם. ולמען זה, הטביע השי״ת השם יתברך, בכללות ההמון, ג' הנטיות, שנקראים קנאה, ותאוה, וכבוד, שבחמתם מתפתח ההמון דרגה אחר דרגה, להוציא מקרבו פני אדם שלם.

## Greed and Honor

(3-8) For example, through the quality of Desire (Greed), they emerge out of the masses because the best of them—those who are endowed with strong will as well as desire—excel in obtaining riches, which represent the first degree of the development of the masses. And just like the Vegetative stage in the whole of reality is governed by external forces that then guide it to its qualities, so, too, the power of Desire in the Speaking species [humanity] is a foreign power, for it is borrowed from the Animal species.

(3-9) And through the quality of [lit. tendency towards] Honor, the heroes and people of fame emerge. They are the ones who govern in synagogues and in towns, etc. And those among them who have a particularly strong will and desire, and also a tendency towards Honor, excel in their ability to obtain governing power, and they represent the second degree of the development of the masses. And this is just like the level of the Animal in the whole of reality, where the power that acts within them is already present in their own essence by themselves, as was mentioned above (3-9). After all, a tendency towards Honor—and with it the desire to govern—is something unique to the human species, as was said in the Scripture: "You have put all things under his feet." (Psalms 8:7)

## Jealousy

(3-10) And through the tendency towards Jealousy, the men of wisdom emerge from [the masses], as was said by our sages, "Jealousy among the scribes increases the wisdom in the world." (Tractate *Bava Batra*, 21a) This is because strong-willed people who are endowed with the quality of Jealousy are found to excel in attaining wisdom and learning; they are just like the stage of the Speaking species in the whole of reality because the active power within them is not limited to time and space, but is general and comprehensive with regard to all the details both of the world and of all times, as mentioned above (3-4).

## תאווה וכבוד

(ג-8) והנה ע"י על ידי נטיית התאוה, מוציאים מתוכם את העשירים, שהמובחרים מהם ברצון חזק, וגם תאוה להם, נמצאים מצטיינים בהשגת העשירות, שהמה דרגה הראשונה להתפתחות ההמון, ובדומה לדרגת הצומח, שבכלל מציאות, אשר כח נכרי מושל עליהם, להנטותם לסגולותם, שהרי כח התאוה במין האדם, כח זר הוא, ומושאל ממין החי.

(ג-9) וע"י ועל ידי נטיית הכבוד, מוציאים מתוכם את הגבורים אנשי השם, המה המושלים בבית הכנסת, ובעיר וכדומה, שבעלי רצון החזק שבהם וגם נטיית הכבוד להם נמצאים מצטיינים בהשגת ממשלה, והמה דרגה הב' להתפתחות ההמון, ובדומה לדרגת מין החי שבכלל המציאות, אשר כח הפועל שבהם, כבר מצוי במהותם בפני עצמם, כאמור לעיל (ג-3) שהרי נטיית הכבוד, נבדלת היא למין האדם בפני עצמו, ועמה חפץ הממשלה, כמו"ש כמו שכתוב כל שתה תחת רגליו (תהילים ח', ז').

## קנאה

(ג-10) וע"י ועל ידי נטיית הקנאה מוציאים מתוכם את החכמים, כמש"א כמה שאמרו ז"ל קנאת סופרים תרבה חכמה (בבא בתרא, דף כא', עמוד א'), שבעלי רצון חזק, ונטיית הקנאה להם, נמצאים מצטיינים בהשגת חכמה ומושכלות, ובדומה, לדרגת מין המדבר שבכלל המציאות, אשר כח הפועל שבהם, בלתי מוגבל בזמן ומקום אלא כללי ומקיף לכל פרטי העולם, ולכל הזמנים, כאמור לעיל,(ג-4).

(3-11) And this is the nature of the flame of jealousy: It is all-inclusive and comprehensive regarding the whole of reality and for all times. This is the rule regarding jealousy: Had [a person] not seen that certain object at his friend's, the craving for it would have not arisen at all. Thus, it turns out that the feeling of lack [in a person] does not arise out of [his] actually lacking something, but out of what his friends have, meaning all descendants of Adam and Eve through all the generations. Therefore, there is no limit to this motivating power, and this is why it is fit for its exalted and high role.

## The Beneficial Power and Harmful Power are the Same

(3-12) Indeed, the reason for those who remain without a prominent virtue is because they do not have a strong will, and therefore, the above three qualities are mixed together within them. Sometimes they are subject to a desire, sometimes they are jealous, and sometimes they want honor. And so their desire is shattered into pieces, and they are like little children who wish for whatever they see, yet do not succeed in anything. They achieve nothing! Therefore, their value is like that of the straw and bran that is left after the flour [is produced].

(3-13) It is known that beneficial power and harmful power are the same [force]. That is to say, as much as such power is able to benefit [a person], so, too, is it able to cause harm. Therefore, because one single human being is more powerful than all the beasts and animals of all generations and all times, as mentioned above (3-5), his ability to harm is more than all of theirs [put together].

(3-14) Therefore, as long as the human is not fit for his exalted rank—in that he will use his power only for beneficial purposes—he needs to take extra restriction so that he will not gain too much of the virtue of humans, which is wisdom and knowledge. It is for this reason that the early men of wisdom [sages] hid the Wisdom [of Kabbalah] from the masses, fearing that they would end up with

(ג-11) וכן מטבע אש הקנאה הוא כללי ומקפת לכל המציאות, ולכל הזמנים כי זהו משפט הקנאה, שבאם שלא הי' היה רואה זה החפץ אצל חברו, לא הי' היה מתעורר לחשוק אלי' אליו כל עיקר, ונמצא שאין הרגשת החסרון מתוך מה שחסר לו, אלא מתוך מה שיש לחבריו, שהמה כל בני אדם וחוה, מכל הדורות, אשר ע"כ על כן, אין קצה לכח הפועל הזה, וע"כ ועל כן מוכשר לתפקידו הנשא והנעלה.

## התועלת והנזק שווים בכוחם

(ג-12) אמנם הנשארים בלי שום סגולה, היא, מפני שאין להם רצון חזק, וע"כ ועל כן כל ג' הנטיות הנזכרים, משמשים להם יחד בערבוביא, לפעמים מתאוים, ולפעמים מתקנאים, ולפעמים חושקים כבוד, ורצונם נשבר לרסיסים, ודומים לקטנים, שכל מה שרואים חושקים, ולא יעלה בידם, מהשגה של כלום, ולפיכך יהי' יהיה ערכם כמו קש וסובין, הנשארים אחרי הקמח.

(ג-13) ונודע שכח המועיל וכח המזיק, עולים בקנה אחד, כלומר, כמה שמסוגל להועיל, כן מסוגל להזיק, ולפיכך כיון שאדם פרטי אחד, עולה כחו על כל הבהמה והחי מכל הדורות והזמנים כנ"ל כנראה לעיל, (ג-5) כן כח המזיק שבו עולה על כולנה.

(ג-14) וע"כ ועל כן כל עוד שאינו ראוי למעלתו, באופן שישמש בכחו רק להועיל, לשמירה יתרה הוא צריך, שלא יקנה מדה מרובה ממעלת האדם, שהיא החכמה והמדע. ולמען זה הסתירו החכמים הראשונים את החכמה, ממרחבי ההמון, מפחד שלא יארע להם תלמידים שאינם הגונים, וישמשו עם כח החכמה, להרע ולהזיק,

unsuitable students who would misuse the power of this wisdom to do evil and cause harm; [indeed,] they could explode with their beastly desire and ferociousness, augmented by their great human power, and destroy the whole world.

## Two Worlds: Materialistic and Spiritual

(3-15) And since there has been a decline in [the standards of] the generations, with even the men of wisdom starting to feel a desire for both worlds, [lit. tables]—namely, for a good life [to their materialistic inclinations as well—therefore, their thoughts have started to approach those of the general masses, and they have started trading with them and have sold the Wisdom [of Truth] for "the fee of a prostitute and at a price of a dog." (Deuteronomy 23:19)

(3-16) And since then, the fortified wall, upon which the first sages based everything, was destroyed. The masses stole the Wisdom [of Truth] for themselves, and the savages filled their hands with the power of the people and they took hold of the Wisdom and tore it apart. Half of it was inherited by the fornicators, and half of it by the murderers, and they have shamed and disgraced it forever, and so it remains to this day.

ונמצאים פורצים בתאותם ופראיותם הבהמית, בכחו הגדול של האדם, ויחריבו את הישוב כולו.

### שני שולחנות: גשמיות ורוחניות

(ג-15) ואחר שנתמעטו הדורות, וחכמיהם בעצמם החלו לחשוק לשני שולחנות, לאמור לחיים טובים גם לחומריותם, ולכן נתקרבה דעתם גם לההמון, ויסחרו עמהם, ומכרו החכמה באתנן זונה ובמחיר כלב (דברים כג', יט').

(ג-16) ומאז נהרס החומה הבצורה, אשר שתו עליה הראשונים, ויחמסוה להם ההמונים, והפראים, מלאו ידיהם בכח אנשים, והחזיקו בחכמה ויקרעו אותה, חציה ירשו המנאפים, וחציה למרצחים, וישימוה לחרפה לדראון עולם, כיום הזה.

# Chapter 4: The Revelation of the Wisdom in Times of Messiah

## Concealing the Wisdom

(4-1) From this, you can judge the Wisdom of Truth, which includes all the [branches of] secular [lit. external] wisdom, for they are her [the Torah's] seven young maidens (*Zohar, Pikudei* 749), as it is well known; and this is the completeness of the human species and the purpose for which all the Worlds were created. As it was said: "If My covenant of day and night [stand not, and] if I have not appointed the ordinances of Heaven and Earth…" (Jeremiah 33:25)

(4-2) Therefore, our sages put boundaries [by saying]: "He who exploits the crown [of Torah for personal benefit] will fade away" (*Pirkei Avot* 4:5); see there. They forbade us completely to use her [the Torah] for even a little joy for oneself alone [lit. for the life of the flesh]. This [boundary] is what has helped us to this very day to strengthen ourselves with might and with shield and to defend the Wisdom of Truth and not allow any stranger and outsider to break in and enter inward. Also, [this boundary] did not allow anyone to grab it and put it in their satchel to go out and trade it in the marketplace, as in the case of the external [secular] men of wisdom. All those who have entered [the Wisdom of Truth] have been subject to a sevenfold examination to the point that [kabbalists] could be sure that they were trustworthy beyond any suspicion or worry whatsoever.

## Opening the Fountains of the Wisdom

(4-3) After these words of truth, [however,] we find a seemingly great and complete contradiction from beginning to end in the words of our sages. We find in the *Zohar* that right before the Messiah comes,

# פרק ד: גלוי החכמה בימות משיח

## הסתרת החכמה

ד-1 ומזה תשפוט לחכמת האמת, אשר כל החכמות החיצוניות כלולים בתוכה, שהמה שבע נערותיה הקטנות (זוהר, פקודי תשמ"ט), כנודע, והוא שלימות מין האדם, והמטרה שכל העולמות בשבילה נבראו, כמ"ש כמו שכתוב אם לא בריתי יומם ולילה חוקות שמים וארץ לא שמתי, (ירמיהו, לג, כה).

(ד-2) אשר ע"כ על כן גדרו לנו חז"ל (אבות ד' משנה ה'), דאשתמש בתגא חלף, המשתמש בכתר [תורה] יחלוף [מן העולם] ע"ש עיין שם, כי אסרו לנו להנות בסיבתה, הנאה של כלום לחיי הבשרים. והיא שעמדה לנו עד היום הזה, להחזיק בחיל וחומה, על חכמת האמת, וכל נכרי וזר, לא יתפרץ להיכנס אליה פנימה, גם לא ישמו בכליהם, לצאת ולסחור עמה בשוק, במקרה החכמים החיצונים כי כל הנכנסים כבר נבדקו בשבע בדיקות, עד שהי' היו בטוחים מכל חשש וחשד של כלום.

## פתיחת מעינות החכמה

(ד.3) ואחר הדברים והאמת הזה, אנו מוצאים לכאורה, סתירה גדולה מקצה אל הקצה, בדברי חז"ל, דאיתא מובא בזוהר דבעקבתא דמשיחא עתידא חכמתא דא להתגלות בימות משיח עתידה חוכמה זו

this Wisdom [of Truth] is destined to be revealed even to youngsters. According to that, we learn that right before [the Coming of] the Messiah, the entire generation will achieve a complete height, so [this wisdom] will not need any protection. The Fountains of this Wisdom will open to quench the thirst of an entire nation. Yet in Tractate *Sotah* 49 and in Tractate *Sanhedrin* 97a, the sages say that right before the Coming of the Messiah, "impudence [lit. *chutzpah*] will increase, etc., the Wisdom of the Scribes will be corrupt, etc., and those who fear sin will be despised, etc."

(4-4) This explains clearly that there is no other generation equal to [this pre-Messianic one] in its evil. How, then, can these two statements be reconciled? Surely, both these statements are the living words of the Creator. The point is that all the exceptional protection and the locking of the doors to the Halls of Wisdom is due to a fear of those people in whom the spirit of "jealousy among scribes" is mixed with the power of selfish desire and honor, and their jealousy is not limited only to the pursuit of wisdom and knowledge. So by this, [it is evident] that the two statements are both correct, as one teaches about the other.

## Opening the Gates of Kabbalah

(4-5) Because "the face of the generation is like the face of a dog," which means that people are crying out "arf, arf" (Heb. *hav, hav*, which also means give, give) like a dog, and those who fear sin will be despised, and the wisdom of the sages will be corrupt. (Tractate *Sanhedrin* 97a) In any case, it is permitted to open wide the Gates of the Wisdom and to remove the careful guarding because [the Wisdom of Truth] is by itself safe from exploitation and robbery.

(4-6) There is no longer any fear that a coarse and unsuitable student will take it to sell in the market to the materialistic masses because no buyers will be found for this merchandise, as it is already despised by them. And because there is no longer [any] hope of fulfilling any selfish desires and obtaining honor through [this Wisdom], it has

להתגלות, אפי' אפילו לצעירי ימים. אשר לפי האמור נמצינו למדים, שבעקבתא דמשיחא, יהי' יהיה כל הדור ההוא בתכלית הגובה, עד שאין אנו צריכים לשום שמירה, ויתפתחו מעיינות החכמה, להשקות כל הגוי כולו. אמנם במס' סוטה [דף] מ"ט וסהנדרין [דף] צ"ז ע"א עמוד א' אמרו ז"ל דבעקבתא דמשיחא בימות משיח חוצפה יסגא וכו' חכמת הסופרים תסרח וכו' ויראי חטא ימאסו וכו'.

(ד.4) והנה מפורש שאין עוד כדור הזה לרוע ואיך מכלכלים לב' המאמרים האלה שודאי אלו ואלו דברי אלהי"ם חיים. והענין הוא, כי כל שמירה המעולה, ונעילת הדלת על היכל החכמה, הוא, מפחד האנשים שרוח קנאת סופרים שבהם, מעורב בכח התאוה, והכבוד, ואין קנאתם מוגבלת, בחפץ החכמה ומושכלות לבד. ובזה נמצאים ב' המאמרים הנ"ל צדקו יחדיו, שבא זה ולימד על זה,

### הסרת השמירה

(ד.5) כי מאחר שפני הדור כפני הכלב, כלומר שצוחין ככלבא הב הב, ויראי חטא ימאסו, וחכמת חכמים תסרח בהם (שם), ממילא מותר להרחיב שערי החכמה, ולהסיר השמירה המעולה, להיותה בטוחה מאלי' מאליה, מחמס ועושק.

(ד.6) ואין עוד פחד מתלמיד שאינו הגון, שיטול אותה למכור בשוק, להמון עם, החומרים, היות שלא ימצא להם קונים על סחורה זו, כי כבר נמאסת בעיניהם, וכיון שאין עוד תקוה לנחול תאוה וכבוד

thereby become safe and is automatically protected. No strangers, except for the real lovers of this Wisdom and understanding, will even approach it. Therefore, no examination should be performed on those who enter [the Wisdom], to the point that even those who are young in years could merit to obtain it.

(4-7) Through this, you will come to understand what [the sages] said: "The Son of David [the Messiah] shall come only [in a time] in which the entire generation is innocent or the entire [generation] is guilty." (Tractate *Sanhedrin*, 98a) But this is very perplexing because it seems that as long as there are a few innocent people in that generation, they would be delaying the Redemption. Does it mean that only when all the innocent people perish from the face of the earth, Heaven forbid, it would be possible for the Messiah to come? I wonder.

## Perfection of Divine Perception and Knowledge

(4-8) We have to understand very deeply that the idea of the Redemption and the Coming of the Messiah that we hope for— may it come soon in our days—is the purpose of the height of the perfection of Divine Perception and Knowledge, as is said: "For they shall all know Me, from the smallest of them to the greatest." (Jeremiah 31:34) But with the perfection of knowledge comes also the perfection of the bodies, as is written in Isaiah 65:20: "For the child shall die a hundred years old, etc."

(4-9) And when the Israelites shall achieve the perfection of full knowledge, the wellspring of understanding and knowledge shall flow more forcefully beyond the boundaries of Israel and shall irrigate all the nations of the world, as is said in Isaiah 11:9: "For the Earth shall be full of the knowledge of the Creator as the waters cover the sea," and as it is [further] said, "They shall come [lit. flow] unto the Creator and to His goodness, etc."

על ידיה, נעשית בזה, בטוחה ומשומרת מאליה, שכל זר לא יקרב, זולת אוהבי חכמה ותושי' ותושיה, לבד, ולפיכך יוסר כל בדיקה מהנכנסים, עד שגם צעירי ימים יוכלו לזכות בה.

ד-7 ובזה תבין אמרם ז"ל, במסכת סהנדרין [דף] צ"ח ע"א עמוד א, אין בן דוד בא אלא בדור שכולו זכאי או כולו חייב שתמוה מאוד דכל כמה שימצא איזה זכאים בדור, יהי' יהיו מעכבים הגאולה, אלא יתמו הזכאים חלילה מהארץ, ואז יהי' יהיה היכולת לביאת המשיח, אתמהא.

### שלימות ההשגה והדעת

(ד-8) אמנם צריך להבין מאד מאד, שזה ענין של הגאולה, וביאת המשיח המקוה לנו בב"א במהרה בימנו אמן הוא ענין תכלית הגובה של שלימות ההשגה והדעת כמו"ש כמו שכתוב ולא ילמדו עוד איש את רעהו לדעת את ה' כי כולם ידעו אותי מגדלם עד קטנם וכו' (ירמיהו לא, לג). אלא שעם שלימות הדעת נשלמים גם הגופות כמ"ש כמו שכתוב [בספר] ישעי' ישעיהו פרק ס"ה, פסוק כא, הנער בן מאה שנה ימות וכו'.

(ד-9) וכאשר יושלמו בני ישראל, עם דעת השלם יתגברו מעיינות התבונה והדעת מעל לגבול ישראל וישקו לכל אומות העולם, כמ"ש כמו שכתוב [בספר] ישעי' ישעיהו פרק י"א כי מלאה הארץ דעה את ה' וכו' וכמו"ש וכמו שכתוב וינהרו אל ה' ואל טובו וכו'.

(4-10) This increase of knowledge is the result of the expansion of the kingdom of the Messiah unto all the nations, except for the crude materialistic masses, whose imagination is fixed on the ultimate power of the fist. And therefore, what is imprinted in their imagination is the expansion of the kingdom of Israel over the nations, but only through the kind of control that is related to dominion of "bodies over bodies" in order to grab their earnings with great arrogance and to feel proud over all the people of the world. And what can I do with them if our sages have already rejected all of them and [those] like them from the congregation of the Creator, by saying, "Anyone who becomes arrogant, the Creator says: 'I [the Creator] and he [the arrogant] cannot live together in one place of residence'"? (Tractate *Sotah*, 5)

## Perfected Knowledge and Awareness Precedes a Perfected Body

(4-11) The opposite are the people who [make the] mistake and judge that as the existence of the body necessarily precedes in time the existence of [both] the soul and complete knowledge, therefore the perfection of the body and its needs precede the soul's divine perception and the perfection of attaining knowledge. Hence, a weak body is prevented from reaching perfected knowledge, which is a very bitter mistake, worse than death.

(4-12) The reason for this is because it is not possible at all to imagine a perfect body before one has achieved perfected knowledge [and awareness]. The [body] in itself is a punctured sack and a "broken cistern," so it cannot contain in itself anything of use for itself or for others. But when it has attained perfected knowledge, the body also ascends to perfection side by side with that perfect knowledge. And this applies both to individuals as well as to the collective as a whole. Study all this in the *Zohar*, portion Shalach Lecha, regarding the spies; the *Zohar* has spoken about this in length. Study that well.

(ד-10) והתגברות הדעת הזה הוא ענין התפשטות מלכות המשיח אל כל האומות ולאפוקי ולהבדיל מהמון עם גסי החומר, שלהיות דמיונם דבוק בשלימות כח האגרוף, וע"כ ועל כן נחקק בדמיונם, ענין התפשטות מלכות ישראל על האומות, אך ורק במין שליטה הנוהג מגופות על גופות, ליטול שכרם משלם בגאוה גדולה, להתגאות על כל בני חלד, ומה אעשה להם אם כבר חז"ל דחו כל אותם, וכמותם מקהל ה' באמרם: כל המתגאה אומר הקב"ה הקדוש ברוך הוא אין אני והוא יכולים לדור במדור אחד (על פי מסכת סוטה ה')

## שלמות הדעת קודמת לשלמות הגוף

(ד-11) וכן לאפוקי להבדיל מאותם הטועים, ושופטים דכשם שמציאות הגוף, בהכרח שיהי' יהיה מוקדם בזמן, למציאות הנשמה, והמושכלות השלימות, כך, שלימות הגוף וצרכיו, מוקדמים בזמן להשגת הנשמה, ושלימות המושכלות, באופן שגוף חלש נמנע מהשגת מושכלות שלימות, שזה טעות מרה וקשה ממות.

(ד-12) היות שלא יצויר כלל ועיקר גוף מושלם, בטרם שהשיג דעת השלם, להיותו לפי עצמו, שק מנוקב ובור נשבר, לא יכיל משהו תועלת לא לו ולא לאחרים. זולת, עם השגת הדעת השלימה, שאז עולה גם הגוף לשלימותו עמה בקנה אחד ממש, וזה הדין נוהג בין בפרטים ובין בהכלל יחד, ועיין כל זה, בזוהר פרשת שלח בענין המרגלים שהאריך בזה עש"ה. עין שם היטב.

# Chapter 5: The Gates of the Wisdom are Opening

## Not the Torah, Rather the Light in the Torah

(5-1) With this, you will understand what is said in the *Zohar*: "With [the merit of] this Book [the *Zohar*], the Israelites shall go out of the Exile," (*Zohar, Naso,* 90) and also what is said in many other places; that only by the dissemination of the Wisdom of Kabbalah to the majority of the people shall we merit the complete Redemption. Our sages also said: "The Light in [the Torah] puts the person back on the right path." (Jerusalem Talmud, Tractate *Hagigah,* 7a)

(5-2) They were very precise there to instruct us that only the Light within her—"just like apples of gold inside silver ornaments" (Proverbs 25:11)—contains the quality that can bring a person back to the right path because neither the individual nor the nation can fulfill the purpose for which they were created except through the perception of the inner part of the Torah and its secret.

(5-3) Although the complete [revelation of the] knowledge is due to occur [only] when our Righteous Messiah comes, yet it is still written: "He bestows wisdom upon the wise, etc." (Daniel 2:21) and says: "In the hearts of all who are wise-hearted, I have put wisdom." (Exodus 31:6) Therefore, we first need a wide dissemination of the Wisdom of Truth among the people so that we will deserve receiving the benefit from our Righteous Messiah. Consequently, these [two]— the Coming of the Messiah and the dissemination of the Wisdom [of Truth]—are mutually dependent. Understand this well.

## A Generation that is Entirely Innocent or Guilty

(5-4) And this being the case, we have an obligation to establish [Kabbalah] academies and to write books to hasten the dissemination

# פרק ה: מדוע נפתחים שערי החכמה

## לא התורה אלא המאור שבה

(ה-1) ובזה תבין מש"כ מה שכתוב בזוהר דבחבורא דא יפקון בני ישראל מגלותא בספר הזה [הזוהר] יצאו בני ישראל מן הגלות (זוהר, נשא סעיף צ'), וכן עוד בהרבה מקומות, שאך ורק בהתפשטות חכמת הקבלה ברוב עם, נזכה לגאולה השלמה, וכן אמרו חכמינו ז"ל המאור שבה מחזירו למוטב (תלמוד ירושלמי, חגיגה א, ז,).

(ה-2) ודקדקו זה בכונה גדולה להורותינו דרק המאור שבתוכיותה, כתפוחי זהב במשכיות כסף (משלי כה, יא), בה צרורה זו הסגולה, להחזיר האדם למוטב, דהן היחיד והן האומה, לא ישלימו הכונה, שעליה נבראו, זולת בהשגת פנימיות התורה וסודותיה,

(ה-3) והגם ששלימות הדעת מקוה לנו, בביאת משיח צדקינו, אמנם כתיב יהיב חכמתא לחכימין וכו'(דניאל ב', כא') ואומר ובלב כל חכם לב נתתי חכמה, (שמות לא', ו') וע"כ ועל כן להתפשטות גדול של חכמת האמת בקרב העם, אנו צריכין מקודם, באופן שנהי' נהיה ראוים לקבל התועלת ממשיח צדקינו, ולפיכך תלוים המה התפשטות החכמה וביאת משיח צדקנו זה בזה, והבן היטב.

## דור שכולו זכאי או כולו חייב

(ה-4) וכיון שכן הרי אנו מחוייבים לקבוע מדרשות ולחבר ספרים, כדי למהר תפוצת החכמה במרחבי האומה, ולא הי'

of the Wisdom [of Truth] throughout the nation. This was not so in the past because there was the fear of getting a mixture of students [that included those] who were not suitable, as we [have] explained at length above. And due to our many sins, this [namely, not studying Kabbalah] became the main reason for the extension of the time of remaining in the Exile to this very day. This is what was meant by our sages [saying]: "The Son of David [the Messiah] shall come only [in a time] in which the entire generation is innocent [or when the entire generation is guilty]." (Tractate *Sanhedrin*, 98a)

(5-5) ["When the entire generation is innocent,"] that is, where everybody has renounced [their] chase after selfish desires and honor because then it would be possible to establish schools [for studying the Wisdom of Truth] among the masses and to prepare the public for the Coming of the Messiah, the Son of David, as stated above. "Or when the entire generation is guilty," that is, in a generation where the face of the generation is like the face of a dog, where those who fear sin are despised and the wisdom of the scribes will be corrupt in them, etc. (Tractate *Sanhedrin*, 97a).

## No Fear and Worry

(5-6) Then it will be possible to remove the extra precaution, and everyone who remains in the House of Jacob and whose heart beats to attain the Wisdom [of Truth] and the ultimate purpose [of Creation] will be named a holy one. And [such a person] will come and learn because there is no longer any fear and worry that he might not keep his good virtues and [that he might] start trading this Wisdom in the marketplace.

(5-7) This is because among the masses, there is no longer anyone interested in buying it; in their eyes, this Wisdom is considered despicable since nothing can be obtained in return—no [fulfillment of] selfish desire and no honor. Therefore, anyone who wishes to enter [the Wisdom of Truth] may enter. And many shall roam, but

היה כן בזמן הקודם מפני היראה מתערובת תלמידים שאינם מהוגנים, כמו שהארכנו לעיל, וממילא היה זה לעיקר הסיבה של אריכת הגלות בעוה"ר בעונותינו הרבים עד היום הזה, והיינו שאמרו חז"ל: "אין משיח בן דוד בא אלא בדור שכולו זכאי [או בדור שכולו חייב]" (סנהדרין צח ע"א).

(ה-5) ["בדור שכולו זכאי"]: היינו שכולם יהי' יהיו פרושים מרדיפה אחר התאוה והכבוד, שאז יהי' יהיה אפשר לקבוע מדרשות ברבים, להכים לביאת מב"ד משיח בן דוד כנ"ל. "או בדור שכולו חייב" דהיינו בדור כזה, שפני הדור הוא כפני הכלב, ויראי חטא ימאסו, וחכמת סופרים תסרח בהם וכו' (מסכת סוטה דף מ"ט ומסכת סהנדרין דף צ"ז)

### אין חשד ופחד

(ה-6) אשר אז לאידך גיסא, יהי' יהיה אפשר להסיר השמירה היתרה, וכל הנשאר בבית יעקב ולבו דופק להשגת החכמה והתכלית, קדוש יאמר לו ויבוא וילמוד כי אין עוד חשד ופחד, פן ואולי לא ישאר עומד על מדותיו ויצא ויסחור אותה בשוק.

(ה-7) כי כבר אפס קונה מההמון כולו, וכבר החכמה מאוסה בעיניהם באופן שאין להשיג תמורתה, לא תאוה ולא כבוד, ולפיכך כל הרוצה לכנוס יבוא ויכנוס. וישוטטו רבים ויתרבה הדעת בכל

the knowledge shall increase among all those who are worthy of it. In this way, we shall soon merit the Coming of our Righteous Messiah, and the Redemption of our souls, speedily in our days, Amen.

## "I Have Not Added Anything to the Words of My Teachers"

(5-8) By means of the words above, I have removed from myself a major criticism about the fact that I have dared [to expand on this subject] more than any of my predecessors and that in this book, I have uncovered the foundations of the Wisdom [of Truth] that are customarily concealed. [Indeed,] until now, no one has gone this far, meaning [revealing] the essence of the Ten *Sefirot* and all the rules concerning them: The Direct (Light) and Returning (Light); the Inner (Light) and Surrounding (Light); and the secret of the Striking [by Binding] and the secret of the Purification.

(5-9) [Concerning all of these matters,] the authors who preceded me purposefully scattered bits of information here and there, using very subtle hints, in such a way that no human being would be capable of pulling them together. But I, by the Light of the Creator that has shone upon me, and with the help of my teachers, have gathered [this information], and I have revealed things with sufficient explanation and in their spiritual essence beyond space and beyond time.

(5-10) There could have been some major criticism issued against me, [but] what is then the advantage? If there is no additional [information] here on top of the words of my teachers, then Rav Isaac Luria (the Ari) and Rav Chaim Vital, themselves and the authentic commentators of their words, could have revealed and explained these matters in a very open manner, as I have done. And if you wish to say that these matters were, in fact, clear in their [the Ari's and Rav Vital's] minds, then who is this author [Rav Ashlag], who surely would have considered it a great merit to be the dust and ashes under their feet, to say that his [Rav Ashlag's] lot has been better than theirs?

אותם הכדאים לה, ובזה נזכה בקרוב לביאת משיח צדקינו ופדות נפשינו בב"א במהרה בימנו אמן.

## "לא חדשתי ולא הוספתי על רבותי"

(ה-8) ועפ"י ועל פי הדברים האלה, הסרתי מעלי טענה גדולה, בזה שהרהבתי מכל הקודמים אותי, ובאתי בספרי זה, בגילוי יסודות החכמה שדרכן לכסות, שעד הנה לא עבר בה אדם עוד, דהיינו מהות העשר ספירות לכל משפטיהם, בישר וחוזר, ופנימי ומקיף, וסוד ההכאה, וסוד ההזדככות.

(ה-9) אשר המחברים שקדמוני, בכונה פזרו הדברים הנה והנה, וברמיזות דקות, באופן שידו של אדם אינו ראוי לקבץ אותם אשר אנכי באורו יתברך שהופיע עלי, ובעזרת רבותי קבצתי אותם, וגיליתי הדברים די באר, ובצביונם הרוחני, למעלה מן המקום ולמעלה מהזמן.

(ה-10) והי' והיו יכולים לבוא עלי בטענה גדולה, ממ"נ ממה נפשך אם אין פה נוספות על רבותי א"כ אם כן האר"י רבי יצחק לוריא ז"ל ורח"ו ורבי חיים ויטאל ז"ל, בעצמם והמחברים האמיתיים מפרשי דבריהם, הי' היו יכולים לגלות ולבאר הדברים בביאור גלוי, כמו שעשיתי אנכי, ואם נפשך לאמר שלפניהם הי' היה גלוי, א"כ אם כן מי הוא המחבר הזה, אשר ודאי, זכות גדול הי' היה לו להיות עפר ואפר תחת כפות רגליהם ז"ל, לומר שנחלתו שפרה לו ה' יותר מנחלתם.

37

(5.11) It is indeed the case that I have not added anything to my teachers' [words], nor have I claimed anything new by this book, as you will see in the reference section. All my words have already been written and inscribed before—in the *Shemoneh She'arim* (*Eight Gates*) and in the *Etz Chaim* (*Tree of Life*) and in the *Mevo She'arim* (*Entrance to the Gates*), all by Rav Isaac Luria (the Ari)—and I have not added even one word. But [the Ari and Rav Vital] aimed at concealing matters, and therefore, they scattered [their insights], putting one part here and another part there.

(5-12) This is because their generation was not yet entirely guilty, and they needed [to take] extra precautions, as I have mentioned above (5-6). Not so with us. Because of our many sins, all the things that our sages said about the days preceding the Coming of the Messiah have come true. And so, in such a generation [as ours], there is no longer any fear about revealing the Wisdom [of Truth], as we have discussed at length above (5-3,4). Therefore, my words are revealed and put in good order.

(ה-11) אמנם כן, לא הוספתי על רבותי, ולא באתי בחדשות כמו שתראה במראה המקומות, ע"י על ידי החיבור, שכל דברי כבר רשום וכתוב, בשמנה שערים, ובעה"ח, ובעץ החיים ומבו"ש ובמבוא שערים מהאר"י ז"ל, ולא הוספתי עליהם אף מילה אחת. אלה המה כיונו לכסות הדברים, וע"כ ועל כן פזרו אותם אחת הנה ואחת הנה.

(ה-12) והוא מפני שדורם לא הי' היה עוד כולו חייב, והי' והיו צריכים לשמירה יתירה, כנ"ל, כנזכר לעיל (ה-6) משא"כ מה שאין כן אנו שבעוה"ר שבעוונותינו הרבים נתקיימה בנו כל דברי רז"ל רבותינו ז"ל האמורים מראש לעקבתא דמשיחא לימות משיח, שבדור כזה שוב אין פחד מלגלות חכמה, כמו שהארכנו לעיל (ה-3, 4), וע"כ ועל כן דברי מגולים ומסודרים.

# Chapter 6: The Thought of Creation

## Tower Full of Goods

(6-1) Now hear me, my sons, because the Wisdom is singing outdoors (Proverbs 1:20) and now from the streets it calls upon you: "Whoever is for the Creator should come to me," (Exodus 32:26) for I am not a trivial thing for you. I am your life and your longevity because you were not created to pursue grain and potatoes, you and your donkeys to eat out of the same trough. And just as it is not the purpose of the donkey to serve all the other donkeys in the world that are equal to it in age, so, too, it is not the purpose of a human being to serve the bodies of all the created beings of the same age as his animalistic body.

(6-2) However, the purpose of the donkey is to serve the human being, who is superior to him, in order to benefit him; and likewise, the purpose of the human being is to serve the Creator and to complete His intention, as Ben Zoma said, (Tractate *Kidushin*, 82b): "All these were only created in order to serve me, and I [was born] to serve my Owner," as it is said: "All of the Creator's actions are for His own sake." (Proverbs 16:4)

(6-3) [This is] because the Creator desires and craves our completion, as it is said in *Beresheet Rabbah*, Chapter 8, regarding the creation of Adam: "The angels said before the Creator, 'What is mankind that You are mindful of him, and the son of man that You do care for him? (Psalms 8:5) Why do you need this trouble?' The Creator told them, 'Why then [does it say] all sheep and oxen (Psalms 8:8) [were created], etc.? What is this similar to? To a king who had a tower full of all the goods of the earth, yet he had no guests. What is the joy of a king who has a tower full, etc.?' They immediately responded by saying, 'Creator, our Lord, how majestic is Your Name in all the earth. (Psalms 8:2) Do what seems to be good to You!'" (end of quote).

# פרק ו: מחשבת הבריאה

## מגדל מלא כל טוב

(ו-1) ועתה בנים שמעו לי, כן החכמה בחוץ תרונה (משלי א' כ'), והנה עתה מרחובות קוראה אליכם מי לה' אלי (שמות לב כו), לא דבר ריק אני מכם, כי אני חייכם ואורך ימיכם, כי לא נבראתם לחזור אחר מעשה דגן, ותפוחי אדמה אתם וחמוריכם באבוס אחד. וכמו שלא יהי' יהיה מטרת החמור לשמש את כל חמורי עולם בני גילו, כן לא יהי' יהיה מטרת האדם, לשמש את כל גופות הבריות בני גילו של גופו הבהמי.

(ו-2) אבל מטרת החמור לשמש האדם הנעלה הימנו כדי להועילו, ומטרת האדם לשמש להש"ת להשם יתברך ולהשלים כונתו כמו שאמר בן זומא (קדושין, דף פב', עמוד ב'): כל אלו לא נבראו אלא לשמשיני, ואני לשמש את קוני, ואומר כל פעל ה' למענהו ( משלי טז', ד').

(ו-3) כי השי"ת השם יתברך חושק ומתאוה אל השלמתינו כמו שאמרו בבראשית רבה פ"ח פרק ח' בדבר בריאת האדם, וז"ל וזה לשונו שהמלאכים אמרו לפניו יתברך, מה אנוש כי תזכרנו ובן אדם כי תפקדנו (תהילים, ח' ד'), הצרה הזאת למה לך, אמר להם הקב"ה, הקדוש ברוך הוא, א"כ אם כן צונה ואלפים למה [נבראו] וכו' (תהילים, ח' ח') למ"ד למה הדבר דומה למלך שהי' היה לו מגדל מלא מכל טוב, ואין לו אורחים מה הנאה למלך שמלאו וכו'. מיד אמרו לפניו, ה' אדונינו מה אדיר שמך בכל הארץ, (תהילים ח' ב') עביד מאי דהניי לך עשה מה שטוב לך עכ"ל, עד כאן לשונו.

**Waiting for the Guests to Come**

(6-4) Seemingly, one should ponder this metaphor—namely, where does this tower that is full of goods stand, since in our time, we would surely fill it with guests even beyond its capacity? Indeed, these words are sincere. You can see that the angels had no complaints against any of the beings created during the six days of Creation, except for the human species, [and that is] because humankind was created in the image of the Creator and is composed of both the higher and the lower [beings]. The angels who saw this were astonished and became alarmed, for how could a spiritual soul, pure and clean, descend from its lofty heights and come to co-habit in this animalistic, filthy [human] body. And [so] they were wondering: Why do You need this trouble?

(6-5) And they received their answer for this [from the Creator]: A tower full of all [types of] goods but empty of guests has already existed for some time, and in order to fill it with guests, the existence of this human, who is composed of both the higher and lower [beings], is required. Hence, it is necessary for the sublime and pure soul to clothe itself with the trouble of this filthy body. And they [the angels] understood this right away and said, "Do whatever seems to be better to You!"

(6-6) And you should know that this tower full of all goods alludes to the entire pleasure and abundance for which [the Creator] has created all beings [to enjoy]. This is according to what our sages have said: "It is the nature of the Good to bestow goodness;" therefore, He created the Worlds in order to fulfill His created beings. (We have spoken about this at length in *Panim Masbirot* [*Welcoming Face*], branch A, and you can study about it there.)

**Fulfill the Created Beings**

(6-7) However, since past and future do not apply to Him, we have to understand that as soon as [the Creator] thought about creating

**מחכים לאורחים**

(ו-4) לכאורה יש להרהר אחר המליצה הזאת, כי איפוא מצוי ועומד, זה המגדל המלא מכל טוב, אשר בזמנינו זה, באמת, שהינו ממלאים אותו אורחים על כל גדותיו. אמנם כנים הדברים, כי הנך רואה שלא טענו המלאכים, על שום בריה בריה מכל הבריות שנבראו בששת ימי בראשית, זולת על מין האדם לבד, והוא להיות נברא בצלם אלהי"ם, ומורכב מעליונים ותחתונים יחד, והמלאכים שראו את זה, כן תמהו ונבהלו, איך נפש הרוחני זכה וברה תרד מרום המעלה, ולבוא ולדור בכפיפה אחת, עם גוף הבהמי המזוהם הזה, והיינו שתמהו הצרה הזאת למה לך.

(ו-5) ולזה הגיע להם התשובה, שמכבר נמצא מגדל מלא מכל טוב, וריקן מאורחים, וכדי למלאותו באורחין, למציאותו של אדם זה, המורכב מעליונים ותחתונים יחד, אנו צריכין, ולסיבה זו, בהכרח שתתלבש הנפש הזכה וברה, בצרה של הגוף המזוהם הזה, ומיד הבינו זה, ואמרו עביד מאי דהניי לך עשה מה שטוב לך.

(ו-6) ותדע שזה המגדל המלא מכל טוב, יורה כללות העונג והטוב, שבשבילו ברא את הנבראים, ע"ד על דרך שאמרו [חכמינו] ז"ל שמדרך הטוב להטיב, וע"כ ועל כן ברא העולמות, כדי להנות לנבראיו. (והארכנו ענינו בפמ"ס בספר פנים מסבירות ענף א' ומשם תדרשנו).

**להיטיב לנבראים**

(ו-7) וכיון שאין ענין עבר ועתיד נוהג בו ית' צריך להשכיל שתיכף כשחשב לברואת נבראים ולהנות אותם תיכף יצאו ונתהוו מלפניו

the created beings and fulfilling them, they immediately emerged and appeared in front of Him, [the beings] themselves together with the abundance and pleasure they were filled with, [just] as He had thought for them. This is what we find in the book *Cheftzi Bah* (*I Desire It*) by Rav Isaac Luria (the Ari): That all the Upper and Lower Worlds are included in the *Ein Sof* (Endless), even before the *Tzimtzum* (Contraction), in the secret of "He and His Name are one." Study this there in chapter 1.

(6-8) The *Tzimtzum* (Contraction), which is the root of the limited Worlds of *Atzilut* (Emanation), *Beriah* (Creation), and *Yetzirah* (Formation), and *Asiyah* (Action) all the way [down] to this world, occurred because of the craving of the totality of the Root-Souls themselves to make their Form most similar to that of the Creator. This is the subject of *devekut* (cleaving), as was explained there [in *Cheftzi Bah*] that *devekut* and separation in spiritual essence are possible only through the attributes of Similarity of Form and Difference of Form.

## Creating the Desire to Receive

(6-9) Now because the Creator wanted to fulfill [His created beings], the desire to receive pleasure was of necessity instilled into the recipients. Because of this, however, their Form became different from that of the Creator because the Form [of receiving] cannot be found in the Creator at all. After all, from whom can He receive? So for the sake of "correcting" this, the *Tzimtzum* (Contraction) and the boundaries were created, all the way until this world emerged as a reality where the soul is clothed inside a physical body. [And now], when [a person] engages [both] in the study of the Torah and with the work for the sake of giving pleasure to his Maker, [his] Form of Receiving would again unite [with the Light] for the sake of Sharing.

יתברך, הם וכל מילואיהם מהעונג והטוב, יחד, כמו שחשב עליהם.
והיינו דאיתא מובא בספר "חפצי בה" מהאר"י ז"ל שכל העולמות
עליונים ותחתונים כלולים בא"ס ב"ה באין סוף ברוך הוא, עוד מטרם
הצמצום בסוד הוא ושמו אחד, ע"ש שם עיין בפ"א בפרק א'.

(ו-8) ומקרה הצמצום, שהוא השורש לעולמות אבי"ע אצילות, בריאה,
יצירה ועשיה המוגבלים עד לעוה"ז לעולם הזה, קרה מפאת כללות שרשי
הנשמות בעצמם, מחשקם להשוות צורתם ביותר להמאציל ית'
שהוא ענין דביקות. כמו שנתבאר שם, שפירוד ודביקות בכל רוחני,
לא יתכן, זולת בערכין של שיווי הצורה, או שינוי הצורה.

## בריאת הרצון לקבל

(ו-9) ומתוך שרצה יתברך להנותם להמקבלים נטבע בהמקבלים בהכרח
הרצון לקבל הנאתם, שבזה נשתנה צורתם הימנו יתברך, להיות
צורה זו אינו נוהגת כלל ועיקר בגדר המאציל ית' דממי יקבל ח"ו
חס ושלום, ולתיקון זה נעשה הצמצום והגבול, עד ליציאת עוה"ז עולם
הזה, למציאות התלבשות נשמה בגוף גשמי, שבהיותו עוסק בתורה
ועבודה ע"מ על מנת להשפיע נ"ר נחת רוח ליוצרו, תשוב צורת הקבלה
להתאחד בעל מנת להשפיע.

(6-10) This is what is meant by the passage: "and cleave to Him, etc." (Deuteronomy 11:22) because then [a person] makes his Form similar to that of his Creator. Similarity of Form is called *devekut* (cleaving) in spirituality, as was said earlier (6-8). And when this *devekut* is achieved in all the parts of the soul to their perfection, the Worlds shall return to the aspect of *Ein Sof* (Endless), as they were before the *Tzimtzum* (Contraction). "And in their land they will inherit double," (Isaiah 61:7) because then [these perfected souls] can receive all the pleasure and goodness that has always been ready for them in the world of *Ein Sof*, as was said (6-7).

(6-11) In addition to this, they are now ready for the real *devekut*—with no Difference of Form whatsoever—because [now] even their receiving is not for their own pleasure but only for the sake of giving pleasure to their Creator. With this, they are Similar in their Form of giving [pleasure] to the Creator. These are things that I have already spoken of at length and with good reasoning in *Panim Masbirot* (*Welcoming Face*); study that well.

(ו-10) והוא שיעור הכתוב ולדבקה בו (לפי דברים יא', כב') וכו' וכולי

כי אז משוה צורתו ליוצרו, אשר שיווי הצורה הוא דביקות ברוחני כאמור (ו-8) וכשנגמר ענין הדביקות, בכל חלקי הנשמה על מילואם, ישובו העולמות לבחי' לבחינת א"ס אין סוף, כמו שהיו מטרם הצמצום. ובארצם ירשו משנה (ישעיה סא' ז'), כי אז יוכלו לשוב ולקבל כל העונג והטוב המוכן להם מכבר בעולם א"ס ב"ה אין סוף ברוך הוא כאמור (ו-7).

(ו-11) ונוסף עוד כי עתה מוכנים לדביקות אמיתי, בלי שינוי צורה כלל, כי כבר גם הקבלה שלהם אינה להנאת עצמם, אלא להשפיע נ"ר נחת רוח ליוצרם, ונמצאים משתוים בצורת השפעה להמאציל יתברך, וכבר הרחבתי דברים אלו בטוב טעם, בפמ"ס בפנים מסבירות בענף א' עש"ה עיין שם היטב.

# Chapter 7: Two Ways of Redemption

## Raising Our Children

(7-1) By this, you can understand what [the sages] have said: That it is a high necessity for the *Shechinah* (Divine Presence) [to descend] to the Lower Levels. (R Bechayei, Exodus 13:8) This saying is indeed very strange, but it is in keeping with what was said in the above *Midrash* (*Beresheet Rabbah,* 8), where it was compared to a king who has a tower full of all [kinds of] goods, yet does not have any guests, although surely he is sitting in expectation of guests, for without them, all these preparations will be of no use and for nothing.

(7-2) It also resembles a great king to whom a son was born when [the king] was already old. And he loved his son very much, and therefore, from the very day the son was born, he thought about him and made a plan and collected all the best books and the best wise men of the country for his [son's] sake. And he constructed a school [to teach] wisdom to [the boy] and gathered all the best builders and constructed chambers of pleasure for him. [The king] collected all the master musicians and singers and erected music halls for [his son], and collected all the best cooks and bakers from all around the country and supplied him with all the delicacies of the world, etc.

(7-3) Now, the son grew and matured, but he turned out to be a fool, having no desire for learning. And he was blind and did not see or feel the beauty of the buildings; he was deaf and could not hear the voices of the men and women singing; and he had diabetes and could not eat anything except coarse bread. It became a source of shame and anger [for the king].

## Way of Repentance and Way of Suffering

(7-4) And this will make it clear to you what [the sages] meant when they interpreted the verse: "I am the Creator; in its due time, I shall

# פרק ז: שתי דרכים לגאולה

## צער גדול בנים

(ז-1) ובזה תבין אמרם ז"ל, אשר השכינה בתחתונים צורך גבוה (ר' בחיי ב"ר אשר, פירוש לתורה: שמ' יג' ח'), שמאמר הזה מתמיה מאוד. אמנם עולה בקנה אחד עם האמור במדרש הנזכר (בראשית רבה ח'), שדימו הענין למלך שיש לו מגדל מלא מכל טוב. ואין לו אורחים, אשר ודאי, לאורחים יושב ומצפה, דאם לא כן, נמצא כל ההכנה ללא הועיל ולתוהו.

(ז-2) וכדומה, למלך גדול שנולד לו בן לעת זקנתו, שהי' היה חביב לו ביותר, וע"כ ועל כן, מיום הולדו חשב בעדו מחשבות, וקבץ כל הספרים והחכמים המצוינים שבהמדינה ועשה בעדו בית מדרש לחכמה, וקבץ כל הבנאים המצוינים ובנה לו היכלי עונג, וקבץ כל בעלי הנגון ושיר ועשה לו בתי זמרה, וקבץ ממיטב המבשלים והאופים שבמרחבי המדינה והמציא לו מכל מעדני עולם וכו'.

(ז-3) והנה נגדל הבן ובא בשנים, והוא סכל, אין לו חפץ במושכלות, והוא סומא אינו רואה ואינו מרגיש, מיופי הבנינים, והוא חרש לא ישמע בקול שרים ושרות, והוא חלה במחלת צוקר סוכרת, אינו רשאי לאכול אלא אלא פת קיבר לבד, והנה כדי בזיון וקצף.

## דרך תשובה ודרך יסורים

(ז-4) ובזה תבין אמרם ז"ל על הפסוק, אני ה' בעתה אחישנה (ישעיה ס, כב) ופירשו במסכת סנהדרין דף צ"ח: לא זכו- בעתה, זכו - אחישנה.

49

hasten it." (Isaiah 60:22) In Tractate *Sanhedrin* 98, they explained, "If they do not merit, then it will be 'in its due time,' if they do merit, then 'I shall hasten it.'" That is because there are two different ways to attain the above-mentioned goal. [The first is] through becoming aware on their own, which is called the Path of *Teshuvah* (Repentance). If they merit this [path], then "I shall hasten it" will occur [in their case], meaning that [for this path], there is no set time, rather when they attain the merit, the Correction will end, of course.

(7-5) But if they do not merit achieving awareness, there is another way, which is called the Path of Suffering, referring to what our sages said (in Tractate *Sanhedrin,* 97): "I will bring upon them a king like Haman, and they will be forced to return to the right path." This means "in its time" because for this [type of repentance], there is a set time.

(7-6) Through this, [the sages] want to show us that [the Creator's] ways are not our ways, etc. (according to Isaiah 55:8) Therefore, [the Creator] will not experience what a human king of flesh and blood will, as mentioned above, who has gone through a lot of bother and has prepared great and rare things for his favorite son, and eventually [the king suffers from all of it]. All his effort and toil is for no purpose and no avail leading to shame, anger, and dismay. The Creator's deeds, on the other hand, are all sure and sound, and deception does not take place in Him, Heaven forbid.

(7-7) And this is what the sages meant when they said, "If they do not merit, [it occurs] in its due time," [that is,] whatever the will does not accomplish, time does. This is said [also] in *Panim Masbirot* (*Welcoming Face*) at the end of section 71a, regarding the meaning of the passage, "Can you send forth lightning, that they may go and say to you, 'Here we are'?" (Job 38:35); see there. The Path of Suffering can purify every deficiency and physical hold until [a person] understands how to pull his head out from the beastly feeding trough so that he can ascend and climb up the steps of the ladder of human happiness and success, as he comes back and cleaves to his root and completes the Intention [of the Creator].

Wow!

היות שיש ב' דרכים להשגת המטרה הנזכרת, או ע"י על ידי תשומת לב מעצמם, שהוא נקרא דרך תשובה, ואם יזכו לזה יקויים בהם אחישנה, כלומר, שאין על זה זמן קצוב, אלא מתי שיזכו יוגמר התיקון, כמובן.

(ז-5) ואם לא יזכו לתשומת לב יש דרך אחר, שנקרא דרך יסורין, ע"ד על דרך שאמרו ז"ל מסכת סנהדרין דף צ"ז: אני מעמיד להם מלך כהמן, ובע"כ ובעל כורחם חוזרים למוטב, והיינו בעתה כי ע"ז על זה יש זמן קצוב.

(ז-6) וירצו בזה. להורות לנו, שלא דרכי ית' דרכינו וכו' (לפי ישעיהו נה' ח'), וע"כ ועל כן לא יארע לו ית' מקרה מלך בו"ד בשר ודם הנ"ל, אשר טרח והכין כ"כ כל כך גדולות ונצורות, בשביל בנו החביב, ולבסוף נמצא מתאנה מכל וכל, וכל הוצאתו וטרחתו לשוא ולתהו לביזיון וקצף, אולם השי"ת השם יתברך כל מעשיו בטוחים ונאמנים, ודין אונאה אין נוהג בו ח"ו חס ושלום,

(ז-7) והיינו שאמרו ז"ל, לא זכו בעתה, ומה שלא יעשה החפץ יעשה הזמן וכמ"ש וכמו שכתוב בפמ"ס בפנים מסבירות סוף ע"א עמוד א, בשיעור הכתוב: התשלח ברקים וילכו ויאמרו לך הנני (איוב לח, לה) ע"ש עיין שם, דיש דרך היסורין שמסוגל למרק כל חוסר וגשם, עדי שיבין, איך מוציאים ראש מתוך האבוס הבהמי, כדי להגביה על ולעלות ולטפס על דרגת סולם האושר וההצלחה האנושית, כי ישוב ויתדבק בשרשו וישלים הכונה.

# Chapter 8: The Writings of the Holy Ari

## Entering the Chamber of the Divine King

(8-1) Therefore, come and understand how much we have to be grateful for to our Ravs who bestow upon us their holy lights and devote their own souls to benefit ours. They station themselves midway between the Path of Harsh Suffering and the Path of *Teshuvah* (Repentance) and save us from the deepest level of hell, which is more difficult than death. [Those Ravs] habituate us to reach the Heavenly delight; to the height of delicacy and pleasure that is our lot [and] which has been prepared and has been waiting for us from the beginning, as we have mentioned earlier. Each and every one of [those Ravs] acts in his own generation according to the intensity of the Light of his Torah and his holiness, and our sages have already stated that there is no generation that does not have people like Abraham, Isaac, and Jacob in it. (*Midrash Beresheet Rabbah*, 74)

(8-2) Indeed, this divine person, Rav Isaac Luria [the Ari], labored and found for us the fullest measure, and he towered miraculously over his predecessors. And if I had a tongue that speaks lofty words, I would praise the day that his wisdom was revealed as a day almost on par with the day that the Torah was given to the Israelites. There are no sufficient words to describe the measure of his holy work on our behalf, for the doors of [spiritual] perception were closed shut, bolted, and locked, and he came and opened them for us in a way that whoever so desires can enter into the chamber of the [Divine] King. All that is required is nothing more than holiness and purity; to immerse [himself] in the *mikveh* (ritual bath), to groom his hair, and to wear clean clothes in order to stand in front of the Supernal Majesty in a fitting manner.

# פרק ח: כתבי האר"י הקדוש

## להכנס להיכל המלך פנימה

(ח-1) ולפיכך בואו והבינו, כמה וכמה יש לנו להחזיק טובה לרבותינו המשפיעים אלינו אורותיהם הקדושים ומוסרים נפשם להטיב לנפשינו, שנמצאים עומדים בתוך, בין דרך היסורים הקשים, ובין דרך תשובה, ומצילים אותנו משאול תחתית הקשה ממות, ומרגילין אותנו להגיענו לשמי עונג, לגובה העידון והנועם שהיא חלקינו, המוכן וממתין עלינו מכל מראש כנ"ל, אשר כאו"א כל אחד ואחד פועל בדורו כפי עוצם אור תורתו וקדושתו, וכבר אמרו ז"ל אין לך דור שאין בו כאברהם יצחק ויעקב (בראשית רבה, פרק ע"ד).

(ח-2) אמנם זה האיש האלה"י רבינו יצחק לוריא ז"ל, טרח ומצא בעדינו מלא מדתו, הגדיל הפליא על קודמיו, ואם הי' היה לי לשון מדברת גדולות הייתי משבח אותו יום, שנגלה חכמתו כמעט כיום אשר נתנה תורה לישראל. אין די מלה בשיעור פעולתו הקדושה בעדינו, כי היו דלתי ההשגה נעולים בדלתים ובריח, ובא ופתחם אלינו, באופן, שכל מי שמשתוקק לכנוס להיכל המלך פנימה, אין צריך כי אם קדושה וטהרה ולילך למרחץ, ולגלח שערו וללבוש בגדים נקיים, כדי לעמוד לפני המלכות העליונה, כיאות.

## Father of Wisdom Yet Young in Age

(8-3) And you can see how [the Ari], at the age of 38 years, surmounted with his holy wisdom all of his predecessors, including the *Gaonim* and more. Moreover, all the elders of the land, the leaders among the shepherds, and the friends and students of the divine sage Rav Moshe Cordovero [the teacher of the Ari] got up and stood in front of him [the Ari] as students before a Rav. So, too, all the men of wisdom of the following generations to this very day, without anyone missing, [have] abandoned all the books and texts that were composed before him [the Ari], including the Kabbalah of Rav Moshe Cordovero as well as the Kabbalah of the first generations and that of the *Gaonim*, of blessed memory, and they all attached the life of their spirit exclusively to his [the Ari's] sacred wisdom. And it goes without saying that such an absolute victory as this father of wisdom gained, [while] yet young in age, does not come for no reason.

(8-4) But much to our sorrow, the actions of Satan have been successful, and obstacles have been placed in the way of the spreading of his [the Ari's] wisdom throughout the holy people, and only few started to master them. This was mainly because his [the Ari's] teachings were written down by hearsay because every day he taught the Wisdom [of Kabbalah] in front of these students, who were already advanced in years and very well versed in understanding the *Zohar* and the *Tikkunim* (Corrections). In most cases, his holy words were set in order according to the deep questions that they asked—every [student] according to his [personal] interest—and therefore, he [the Ari] did not pass on the wisdom according to a methodical order like the previous compositions that preceded his.

## Order With No Logic

(8-5) We find in his writings that the Ari himself was eager to put everything in order, and you can see this in the short introduction by Rav Chaim Vital to the *Gate of the Articles of Rav Shimon bar*

## אב בחכמה ורך בשנים

(ח-3) והנך מוצא בן ל"ח שנה, הכריע בחוכמתו הקדושה לכל
קודמיו עד הגאונים ועד בכלל. וכל ישישי ארץ אבירי הרועים
חברים ותלמידים של החכם האלה"י הרמ"ק (האלקי רבינו משה
קורדוביירו) ז"ל, קמו עמדו לפניו, כתלמידים לפני הרב, וכן כל חכמי
הדורות, אחריהם, עד היום הזה, איש מהם לא נעדר, משכו ידיהם
מכל הספרים והחיבורים שקדמוהו, הן קבלת הרמ"ק, והן קבלת
הראשונים וקבלת הגאונים, זכר כולם לברכה, וכל חיי רוחם הדביקו
בחכמתו הק' הקדושה ביחוד. ומובן מעצמו שלא על חנם זוכין לנצחון
מוחלט, כמו שנחל אב החכמה ורך השנים הזה.

(ח-4) אולם לדאבון לבינו הצליח מעשה שטן, ונעשו מעקשים בדרך
התפשטות חכמתו למרחבי עם קדוש, ומעוטא דמעוטא, החלו
לכבוש אותם. והוא בעיקר מפני שהדברים נכתבו מפי השמועה,
כמו שדרש בחכמה יום יום לפני תלמידיו שכבר היו ישישי ימים,
ובקיאים גדולים בהשגת הזהר ותיקונים ועל פי רוב נערכו אמרותיו
הקדושים, לפי השאלות העמוקים שהי' היו שואלים הימנו כל אחד
לפי ענינו, ועל כן לא מסר החכמה על הסדרים הראוים, כמו בשאר
החיבורים שקדמו אליו.

## סדר לא הגיוני

(ח-5) ואנו מוצאים בכתבים שהי' היה האר"י ז"ל עצמו משתוקק
לזה לעשות סדר בענינים, ועי' ועיין זה בשער מאמרי רשב"י (רבי שמעון
בר יוחאי) בפירוש האדרא זוטא, בהקדמה קצרה של הרח"ו (רבי חיים

*Yochai* in the *Idra Zuta* commentary. What added to this was the short period of his [Rav Vital] teaching. The entire timespan of teaching his students was about 17 months, as was explained in *The Gate of Reincarnation*, chapter 8. This stated that he arrived in Safed from Egypt in the year 5331 after the Creation (1571 CE), close to the time of Passover, at which time Rav Chaim Vital was 29 years old. In the year 5332 (1572), on Friday, eve of the Sabbath of the Torah portion of Matot-Masei, on the first day of the month of *Av*, [the Ari] fell ill; and on the Tuesday of the weekly portion of Devarim (Deuteronomy), which was the fifth day of [the month] of *Menachem-Av* (Leo), he [the Ari] departed for the life in the World to Come; study there.

(8-6) Furthermore, we [also] find there in chapter 8, that on his deathbed, [the Ari] ordered Rav Chaim Vital to not teach the Wisdom [of Kabbalah] to others. He allowed him only to engage in this study alone and quietly. The rest of the friends were forbidden to engage in this study altogether, saying that they had not understood this Wisdom properly. Look it up there in length. And this is the reason that Rav Chaim Vital did not arrange the writings at all, but left them without order. Furthermore, he did not explain how one matter was connected to another, so that it would not appear that he was teaching [this Wisdom] to others. Thus we find in him an excessive caution in this matter, [something that] is known by those who are familiar with the *Writings of the Ari*.

## Three Different Organizers

(8-7) And those orderly arrangements that we do find in the *Writings of the Ari* were compiled and put in correct order by a third generation [of Ravs] by three different organizers during three periods. The first of these organizers was Rav Yaakov Zemach, who was a contemporary of the great teacher Rav Avraham Azulai, who passed away in 5404 (1644 CE). An important part of the writings had reached Rav Zemach, and he compiled many books from

ויטאל) ז"ל. ונוסף על זה הוא קצרות זמן לימודו כי כל חיי בית מדרשו
הי' היה כ"ז חדשים, כמפורש בש' (שער) הגלגולים שער ח' דף מ"ט,
כי הגיע ממצרים לצפת ת"ו, בשנת של"א ליצירה [1571] קרוב לימי
הפסח, והרח"ו (ורבי חיים ויטאל) ז"ל הי' אז בן כ"ט שנה, ובשנת
של"ב ביום ו' עש"ק ערב שבת קודש פרשת מו"מ מטות ומסעי, בר"ח בראש
חודש מנחם אב נחלה וביום ג' [פרשת] דברים ה' מנ"א מנחם אב, נפטר
לחיי עולם הבא ע"ש עיין שם.

(ח-6) ואיתא ומובא שם עוד בשער ח' דף ע"א עמוד א' שבעת
פטירתו נתן צוואה להרח"ו (רבי חיים ויטאל) ז"ל שלא ילמד את החכמה
לאחרים, ולו התיר לעסוק בה בפני עצמו בלחישה, אמנם לשאר
החברים אסור להתעסק בהם כלל, כי אמר שלא הבינו החכמה
כראוי, ע"ש עיין שם באריכה. והיא הסיבה אשר הרח"ו רבי חיים ויטאל
ז"ל לא סידר כלל את הכתבים, והניחם בלי סדרים, ומכ"ש ומכל
שכן שלא ביאר הקשרים מענין לענין, כדי שלא יהי' יהיה בזה כמו
מלמד לאחרים, ולכן אנו מוצאים הימנו זהירות יתרה בזה כנודע
להבקיאים בכהאר"י בכתבי האר"י ז"ל.

**שלושה מסדרים**

(ח-7) ואלו הסדרים המצויים לפנינו בכתבי האר"י ז"ל, נערכו
ונסדרו ע"י על ידי דור שלישי בג' זמנים, וע"י על ידי ג' מסדרים. הראשון
למסדרים הי' היה החכם מהר"י מורנו הרב יעקב צמח ז"ל, שהי' היה בזמן
אחד עם מהר"א מורנו רבי אברהם אזולאי ז"ל, שנפטר בשנת ת"ד [1644],
שהגיע לידו, חלק חשוב מהכתבים, וסידר מהם הרבה ספרים,

them. The most important of these is *Sefer Adam Yashar* (*The Book of the Upright Man*), in which he gathered the core and the essence of the *Writings* [*of the Ari*] that he had access to. In the introduction to his book *Kol BaRamah* (*A Voice Up High*), Rav Zemach mentions the names of all the books he put together, although some of these books have been lost.

(8-8) The second person to organize [the *Writings the Ari*] was his [Rav Zemach's] sage student, Rav Meir Paprish, who did much more than his Rav (teacher) because some of the books that had belonged to the sage Rav Shmuel Vital had reached him. Rav Paprish compiled many books, the most important of which are *Etz Chaim* (*The Tree of Life*) and *Pri Etz Chaim* (*The Fruit of the Tree of Life*), which contain the entirety of the Wisdom [of Truth] in the full sense of the word.

(8-9) The third organizer was the sage Rav Shmuel Vital, the son of our great teacher and sage Rav Chaim Vital. Rav Shmuel was a great and famous sage, who arranged the famous Eight Gates out of the literary heritage left to him by his father. So we can see that each and every one of these organizers did not have all the writings in their entirety, and that caused a heavy burden in terms of the task of organizing the subjects, which [to this day] are not at all prepared for those who do not have real proficiency in the *Zohar* and in the *Tikunei HaZohar* (*Corrections to the Zohar*). And because of this, people of elevated consciousness are few.

והחשוב מהם, הוא הספר אדם ישר, שאסף בו שורש ועיקר כלל הדרושים מהמצויים לו, ומקצת ספרים שסידר הרב הנ"ל נאבדו, ובהקדמת ספרו קול ברמה, מביא שם כל הספרים שסידר.

(ח-8) מסדר השני הוא תלמידו החכם מהר"מ מורנו הרב מאיר פאפריש ז"ל, והגדיל ביותר מרבו, ז"ל להיות שהגיע לידו, מחלק הכתבים שהי' היה בידי החכם מהר"ש מורנו הרב שמואל וויטאל ז"ל וסידר הרבה ספרים, החשוב מהם, הוא ספר עץ החיים, ופרי עץ חיים, שכוללים מרחבי החכמה, במלוא המובן.

(ח-9) השלישי למסדרים, הוא החכם מהר"ש מורנו הרב שמואל וויטאל ז"ל, בן מוהר"ר מורנו הרב רבי חיים וויטאל ז"ל, והי' היה חכם גדול ומפורסם, הוא סידר שמונה שערים המפורסמים, מעזבון שהניח לו אביו ז"ל. ואנו רואים, שכל או"א אחד ואחד מהמסדרים, לא הי' היה לו כל הכתבים בשלימות, וזה גרם להם כובד גדול על סידורם של הענינים, שאינם מוכשרים כלל לאותם שאין להם בקיאות אמיתי בזוהר ותיקונים, וע"כ ועל כן בני עלי' עליה הם מועטים.

# *Chapter 9: Two is Better than One*

**The Teachings of the Baal Shem Tov**

(9-1) In addition to this, we reserve a special fondness [coming] from the Creator, Who has made it so that we have been worthy of attaining and meriting the spirit of our life—the Baal Shem Tov—whose story of greatness and the power of whose holiness are beyond any utterance and any word. No one has gazed upon him and no one shall gaze upon him except for those who are virtuous and have served under the shine of his light, and even they only [gaze upon him] in proper measure, each and every one according to what he comprehends in his heart. And this is true; that the light of [the Baal Shem Tov's] teachings and his holy wisdom are built on top of holy pillars, especially those of the Ari.

(9-2) However, these two cases are not similar at all, and I will explain it through a parable of someone who is drowning in the river, bobbing up and down as those who drown do. Sometimes only the hair of his head is seen, and then schemes are put together on how to catch him and save him through his head, and sometimes his body is also seen, and then schemes are put together on how to take hold of his body in the area of his heart.

(9-3) So also is this matter, where an Israelite person has been drowning in the turbulent waters of the exile among the nations, from then until now. He is considered to be ascending and descending. But not at all times is it the same. At the time of Rav Isaac Luria, nothing was seen except the head, and therefore, Rav Isaac Luria labored on our behalf to save us by the head. But at the time of the Baal Shem Tov, there was [some] relief, and therefore, it was a blessing for us to save us through the heart, and this has become [our] great and unfailing salvation.

(9-4) But now, due to our many sins, the wheel has turned again, and we have significantly descended, as if from a high peak down

# פרק ט: טובים השניים מן האחד

## קבלת הבעל-שם-טוב

(ט-1) ותמור זה חביבה יתירה מודעת לנו מאתו יתברך שהגיענו וזכינו, לרוח אפינו הבעש"ט הבעל שם טוב ז"ל, אשר פרשת גדולתו ועוצם קדושתו, למעלה מכל הגה ומכל מלה, לא התבוננו ולא יתבוננו בו, זולת אותם הזכאים ששמשו לאורו, וגם הם לשיעורין, כל או"א אחד ואחד לפום מאי דקביל בלבי' לפי מה שליבו יכול לקבל. והן אמת, שאור תורתו וחכמתו הק' הקדושה, נבנים על אדני הקודש מהאר"י ז"ל ביחוד.

(ט-2) אמנם אין ענינם דומה זה לזה כלל, ואסביר זה ע"ד על דרך משל למי שנטבע בנהר, והוא עולה ויורד כדרך הנטבעין, שלפעמים נגלים רק שערות ראשו, ואז מטכסים תחבולות, איך לתופסו ולהצילו דרך ראשו ולפעמים נראה גם גופו ואז מטכסים תחבולות, לתופסו מכנגד לבו.

(ט-3) כן הענין הזה, אחר שאיש ישראל נטבע במים הזדונים גלות העמים, מאז עד עתה, נמצא עולה ויורד, ולא כל הזמנים שום, אשר בזמן האר"י ז"ל לא נראה אלא ראשו, וע"כ ועל כן טרח האר"י ז"ל בעדינו, להצילנו דרך ראש, ובזמן הבעש"ט הבעל שם טוב ז"ל הי' היה הרוחה, וע"כ ועל כן הי' היה לברכה בעדינו, להצילנו מכנגד הלב, והי' היה לנו לתשועה גדולה ונאמנה.

(ט-4) ובעוה"ר ובעונותינו הרבים חזר ונהפך הגלגל בדורינו זה, וירדנו פלאים, כמו מאגרא רמא לבירא עמיקתא (מהר גבוה לבור עמוק), ונוסף

into a deep pit. In addition, there has been war between the nations, which has confused the whole world. And [people's] needs have become great, and the mind has become confined and disrupted by the filth of materialism, which takes the lead, and slaves ride on horses while leaders walk on the ground. And everything that was said in the study portion of the previously mentioned Tractate *Sotah* (page 49) has become true about us because of our many sins.

## Craving

(9-5) And, once again, a wall of iron has been erected to block this great light of the Baal Shem Tov, which we said would go on shining till our complete redemption was achieved. People of wisdom did not believe that there would be a possibility of the coming of a generation that would not see [the Baal Shem Tov's] light, and yet our eyes have lost their vision, and we have lost everything that is good. Seeing this, I said to myself that it is time to take action, and therefore, I have risen to open wide the gates of the light of the Ari, who is the proper and able [channel] for this present generation as well, and two [the Ari and the Baal Shem Tov] are better than one.

(9-6) One should not blame us for the succinctness that is used in my writing because this is adapted to and made fit for all lovers of the Wisdom [of Truth]. After all, too many jars grow weaker the taste of the wine, and a subject can become a burden for the learner. Nor are we responsible for those who are close-minded [lit. whose heart is covered in fat] because the language has not yet been created to assist them, and in every place they lay their eyes upon, there they find an object of their stupidity. There is a rule that the place from which the wise person draws the source of his wisdom is the same place from which the fool draws the source of his foolishness.

(9-7) So on principle, I am standing at the beginning of my book and I declare that I have not labored at all for those who like to look over the chimney tops, but rather for those to whom the word

עלינו התנגשות העמים, אשר בלבל כל העולם כולו, ונעשו הצרכים מרובים, והדעת קצרה, ומשובשה בזוהמת החומר, הנוטל חלק בראש, ועבדים רוכבים על סוסים, ושרים לארץ ילכו, וכל הנאמר במתניתין במס' סוטה (דף מט') הנ"ל נתקיימה בנו בעוה"ר (בעונותינו הרבים).

## השתוקקות

(ט-5) ושוב נעשה מחיצה של ברזל, גם לאור הגדול הזה של הבעש"ט (הבעל שם טוב) ז"ל, אשר אמרנו שהולך ואור עד נכון גאולתינו השלימה, ולא האמינו חכמי לב בהאפשרות בדור יבוא ולא יוכלו לראות לאורו, והנה חשכו עינינו נשינו טובה, ובראותי זה אמרתי עת לעשות, וע"כ (ועל כן) קמתי לפתוח בהרחבה פתחי אורה של האר"י ז"ל, שהוא הוא המסוגל ומוכשר גם לדורינו זה כנ"ל, וטובים השנים מהאחד.

(ט-6) ואין להאשימנו על הקיצור לשון הנוהג בחיבורי, להיות זה מותאם, ומוכשר לכל אוהבי חכמה, כי ריבוי הקנקנים מפיגין טעם היין, ויוכבד המושג על המעיין. ואין אנו אחראין לשמיני הלב, בשעדיין לא נברא הלשון להועילם, ובכל מקום שנותנים עיניהם, מזומן להם חפץ הכסילות, וכללא נקוט, שמאותו מקום שהחכם שואב מקורי חכמתו שואב משם הכסיל מקור אולתו.

(ט-7) ובכלל אני עומד בראש ספרי ומזהיר שלא טרחתי כלל, לכל אותם האוהבים להסתכל בארובות, זולת לאותם שדבר ה' יקר

of the Creator is dear and whose longing to follow the Creator and His goodness keeps on increasing in order to complete the task for which they were created, so that with the Creator's Will, the words of the Scripture—"All those who seek Me diligently shall find Me" (Proverbs 8:17)—will be fulfilled in them.

להם, והולכים ומתגעגעים לנהור אחר ה' וטובו, בכדי להשלים
המטרה שבשבילה נבראו, כי יתקיים בהם ברצות ה' הכתוב כל
משחרי ימצאוני (משלי ח' י'ז) וכו'.

# Chapter 10: The Torah and the People

## A Camel Carrying Silk

(10-1) Come and see the words of the sage Rav Avraham Ibn Ezra [1089–1164] in his book *Yesod Morah* (*Foundation of Awe*) page 8b. And these are his words in section 4: "Now pay attention and know that all the Precepts—whether written in the Torah or accepted by virtue of having been instituted by our forefathers, even though most of them are in action or verbal—are all meant to correct the heart because 'the Creator searches all hearts and understands every plan and thought.' (1 Chronicles 28:9) And it is said: 'To those who are upright in their hearts,' (Psalms 125:4) and the opposite of this is the 'heart that plots wicked plans,' (Proverbs 6:18) and I found one passage that applies to all the Precepts, namely, 'You should be in awe of the Creator your Lord, and you should serve Him.' (Deuteronomy 6:13)"

(10-2) This word "awe" includes in it all the "do not" Precepts in speech, heart, and deed, and this is the first stage from which one ascends to the [spiritual] work with the Creator, which includes all the "do" Precepts. And these ["do" Precepts] will train his heart and guide him until he cleaves to the Creator because this is the purpose for which mankind was created. [A person] was not created to gain wealth and build buildings, etc., and therefore, he should seek everything that would make him love Him [the Creator], learn the Wisdom, and pursue certainty, etc. "And the Creator will open the eyes of his heart and renew in him a different spirit. Then, in his lifetime, he shall become the beloved of his Maker, etc."

(10-3) And you should know that the Torah is only given to people "who have a heart" because words are like corpses but their deeper *ta'am* (taste, meaning) is like the soul, so without understanding the deeper meaning, all of the effort is in vain and the work as useless as hot air. This is like a person who troubles himself to count the pages and number of letters of a medical textbook, although from this labor, he cannot come up with cures. And [this person] is just like a camel that carries silk although [the camel] cannot do any good to the silk, nor can the silk do any good to him; end of quote [of Rav Ibn Ezra], word for word.

# פרק י: התורה והעם

### גמל נושא משי

(י-1) ובא וראה דברי פי חכם, הר"א (הרב אברהם) אבן עזרא ז"ל (1089–1164) בספרו יסוד מורא דף ח' ע"ב, וז"ל (זה לשונו בא"ד באות ד', ועתה שים לבך ודע, כי כל מצוות הכתובות, בתורה או המקובלות שתקנו האבות, אעפ"י (אף על פי) שרובם הם במעשה או בפה, הכל הם לתקן הלב, כי כל לבבות דורש ה', וכל יצר מחשבות מבין (דברי הימים כח, ט) . וכתוב (תהילים רכב, ד), לישרים בלבותם, והפך זה לב חורש מחשבות און וכו' (משלי ו, יח) ומצאתי פסוק אחד כולל לכל המצוות, והוא, את ה' אלהי"ך תירא ואותו תעבוד (דברים ו, יג).

(י-2) והנה מלת "תירא", כולל לכל מצות לא תעשה, בפה ולב ומעשה, וזו היא המדרגה הראשונה, שיעלה ממנה, אל עבודת ה' יתעלה, שהיא כוללת כל מצות עשה, ואלה, ירגלו לבו וידריכוהו, עד כי ידבק בהשם יתברך הנכבד, כי בעבור זה נברא האדם, כי לא נברא לקנות הון ולבנות בנינים וכו' ע"כ (על כן יש לו לבקש כל דבר שיביאנו לאהוב אותו ללמוד חכמה, ולבקש האמונה, וכו', וה' יפקח עיני לבו ויחדש בקרבו רוח אחרת. אז יהי' (יהיה) בחייו אהוב ליוצרו וכו'.

(י-3) ודע כי התורה לא נתנה אלא לאנשי לבב. כי התיבות כגויות, והטעמים כנשמות, ואם לא יבין הטעמים כל עמלו שוא ועמל ורוח, כמו המייגע עצמו לספור הדפין והתיבות שבספר רפואה, שמזאת היגיעה לא יוכל לרפאות מזור, וכמו גמל נושא משי, והוא לא יועיל להמשי, והמשי לא יועילנו, עכ"ל (עד כאן לשונו אות באות.

**Wisdom of the Heart**

(10-4) What we extract from his words is one: Keep our focus on the purpose for which man was created. He [Rav Avraham Ibn Ezra] says about [this purpose] that it is the cleaving to the honorable Creator. And therefore, he says that the person has to pursue the tricks that will bring him to love the Creator, learn the Wisdom [of Truth], and pursue certainty until he merits that the Creator will open "the eyes of his heart" and renew in him a different spirit. Because it is then that he shall become the beloved of his Maker in his lifetime. And he [Rav Ibn Ezra] specifies with great intention that a person must become the beloved of his Maker in his lifetime, indicating that as long as he has not yet merited this asset [of wisdom and certainty], his [spiritual] work is not complete and that the work that has been given to us definitely has to be done today.

(10-5) [Rav Ibn Ezra] concludes by saying that the Torah was given only to people who "have a heart," that is to say, those who have acquired a heart through which they can love [their Maker] and yearn for Him. In the language of the sages, they are called "wise in heart" because they no longer have an animal spirit, which descends downward, since the disposition to the Evil Inclination resides only in a heart that is devoid of wisdom. And he explains further and says that words are like corpses but that their *ta'am* (taste, meaning) is like the soul. If one does not understand the meaning, it is like someone who labors to count the pages and the words in a medical textbook, even though from this kind of labor, one cannot bring cure and relief to others.

**Inner Aspect of the Torah**

(10-6) What he intends to say is that one must of necessity find tools [lit. schemes] to gain the above-mentioned asset because then one can taste the *ta'am* (taste, meaning) of the Torah, which is the subject of the inner Wisdom and its mysteries, as well as the *ta'am* of

## חכמי הלב

(י-4) הנשאב מדבריו ז"ל שהוא באחת, דהיינו לאחוז בהמטרה, שעליה האדם נברא. ואומר עליה, שהיא ענין הדביקות בהשם ית' הנכבד, ואומר ע"כ על כן, שהאדם מחויב לחזור אחר התחבולות, שיביאנו לאהוב אותו, ללמוד חכמה ולחפש אמונה, עדי שיזכה שהש"י שהשם יתברך יפקח עיני לבו, ויחדש בקרבו רוח אחרת, שאז יהיה בחייו אהוב ליוצרו. ובכוונה גדולה מדייק זה שיהי' יהיה בחייו אהוב ליוצרו, להורות, שכל עוד שלא זכה לקנין הזה, אין עבודתו שלימה, והעבודה בהכרח שנתנה לנו היום לעשותם.

(י-5) וכמו שמסיים על זה כי התורה לא נתנה אלא לאנשי לב, כלומר, שהשיגו לב, לאהוב אותו ויחמדהו, שהם נקראים בלשון חכמים חכמי לב להיות שאין שם עוד רוח הבהמי היורד למטה, שאין היצה"ר היצר הרע שורה אלא בלב פני מחכמה. ומפרש ואומר שהתיבות כגויות, והטעמים כנשמות, ואם לא יבין הטעמים, הרי זה דומה למיגע עצמו לספור דפין ותיבות שבספר רפואה, שמזאת היגיעה לא יוכל לרפאות מזור.

## פנימיות התורה

(י-6) רצונו לומר שבהכרח מחוייב למצוא התחבולות, לזכות להקנין הנזכר, שאז מסוגל לטעום טעמי תורה, שהוא ענין החכמה הפנימית ומסתריה, וטעמי מצוה שהוא ענין האהבה והחמדה אליו

the Precepts, which is the love and yearning for Him [the Creator]. For without this [ta'am], a person has only words and deeds, which are corpses without souls. This is like a person who labors counting the pages and the words in a medical text, etc.

(10-7) Surely [knowledge of] medicine cannot be completely obtained before one [actually] understands the meaning of the medical text, even after he goes and buys it with all the money that he was asked to pay for it. And if he does not study things in the proper order of the study and the action is not arranged to bring us to that, then he is like a camel that carries silk without doing any good to the silk, and neither does the silk benefit this person to bring him to the perfected intention for which [he] was created.

ית', שבלעדי זה, נמצא שאין לו, אלא התיבות והמעשים לבד, שהמה גויות בחוסר נשמות, שדומה למייגע עצמו לספור דפין ותיבות שבספר רפואה וכו'.

(7-י) שודאי לא יושלם בו הרפואה, מטרם שמבין פירושה של הרפואה הכתובה, וגם אחר שילך ויקנה אותה בכל הדמים שיפסקו עלי עליו, ואם סדרי הלימוד והמעשה אינם מסודרים להביאנו לזה, דומה לגמל נושא משי שהוא אינו מועיל להמשי, והמשי לא יועילנו להביאו אל שלימות הכוונה שבשבילה נברא.

# Chapter 11: Divine Providence

## Different Camps and Groups

(11-1) From these words, we can attain the "opening of the eyes" [mentioned] in the saying of Rav Simon in *Midrash Rabbah*, chapter 6, about the passage: "Let us make Man," (Genesis 1:6) which says the following, ("As the Creator was about to create Man, He consulted with His Serving Angels,) who were divided into different camps and groups, some of them saying, "Let him be created" and others saying, "Let him not be created." About this, it is written: "Mercy and Truth met, Righteousness and Peace kissed each other." (Psalms 85:11)

(11-2) Mercy said, "Let him be created, for he will perform actions of mercy." Truth said, "Let him not be created, for he is all lies." Righteousness said, "Let him be created, for he does righteousness," and Peace said, "Let him not be created because he is all quarrels." What did the Creator do? He took Truth and threw it to the ground, as it is written: "…and Truth was cast down to the ground." (Daniel 8:12).

(11-3) [Then] the angels said to the Creator, "Why do you disgrace Your Seal? Let Truth rise from the earth." Hence it is written: "Truth will spring up from the ground." (Psalms 85:12) Study that [*Midrash Rabbah*] well.

(11-4) And behold, this story is full of difficulties from all directions: (1) There is still no explanation here regarding the seriousness of the verse: "Let us make Man." Indeed, does [the Creator] need advice, Heaven forbid, as the Scriptures say: "Salvation comes from the heart of a counselor". (Proverbs 11:14) (2) [Regarding] a mouth [that speaks] truth, how can it say here that the entirety of the human species is all lies? After all, there is no generation that does not have people like Abraham, Isaac, and Jacob. (*Beresheet Rabbah*, 74) (3) And if the lips of Truth speak honestly, how is it that the Angels

# פרק יא: השגחה עליונה

### כתות, כתות; חבורות, חבורות

(יא-1) ועפ"י ואף על פי הדברים הללו, השגנו פקיחת עינים במאמר ר' סימון, במדרש רבה פרק ו' על פסוק, נעשה אדם (בראשית א' ו'), וז"ל וזה לשונו: (שבא הקב"ה הקדוש ברוך הוא לבראות את האדם נמלך במלאכי השרת) שנעשו כתות כתות חבורות חבורות, מהם אומרים יברא, ומהם אומרים אל יברא, הה"ד הדא הוא דיכתיב (וזה שכתוב) חסד ואמת נפגשו, צדק ושלום נשקו (תהילים פה, יא).

(יא-2) חסד אמר יברא, שהוא גומל חסדים. אמת אמר אל יברא, שכולו שקרים. צדק אמר יברא, שהוא עושה צדקות, ושלום אמר אל יברא, שכולו קטטה. מה עשה הקב"ה הקדוש ברוך הוא, נטל האמת והשליכו לארץ הה"ד הדא הוא דיכתיב (וזה שכתוב) ותשלך אמת ארצה (דניאל ח,יב).

(יא-3) אמרו מלאכי השרת לפני הקב"ה הקדוש ברוך הוא, מה אתה מבזה תכסיס אלתכסייה (חותם) שלך, תעלה האמת מן הארץ, הה"ד הדא הוא דיכתיב (וזה שכתוב) אמת מארץ תצמח (תהילים פה, יב) עש"ה עין שם [במדרש רבה] היטב.

(יא-4) והנה המאמר הזה מוקשה הוא סביב סביב, א' עדיין לא נתבאר בזה חומר הכתוב דנעשה אדם וכי ח"ו חס ושלום לעצה הוא צריך עד"ה על דרך הכתוב תשועה בלב יועץ (משלי יא', יד'). ב', פה אמת, איך יאמר על כלל מין האדם שכולו שקרים, והא אין לך דור, שאין בו כאברהם יצחק ויעקב (בראשית רבה, פרק ע"ד). ג', ואם כנים שפתי אמת, איך מלאכי חסד וצדקה הסכימו על עולם שכולו שקר. ד', למה נקרא האמת תכסיס אלתכסייה, שפי' חותם, הבא בשולי

of Mercy and Righteousness agree upon a world that is all lies? (4) Why is Truth called a seal—[something that] appears at the end of a letter—which necessarily means that there is a reality of essence other than that of the seal. Indeed, beyond the boundary of truth, there is surely no reality there at all. (5) Is it possible for the Angel of Truth to think that any action by the Performer of Truth [the Creator] is not, Heaven forbid, truthful? (6) Why did Truth deserve this harsh punishment of being cast to the ground and into the ground? (7) Why was the answer of the angels not mentioned in the Torah, as was the question posed to them?

## The Providence the Governs Reality

(11-5) We have to understand these two types of supervision laid out before us and which are polar opposites. They are the supervision of the entire reality of this world, and the supervision of the ways of existence for each and every one to be established in the reality in front of us. From one end, we find reliable supervision, with a most wonderful credible Providence governing each and every creature in existence. And for this purpose we can use, for example, the guidelines of Creation to explain the existence of mankind.

(11-6) We find that man's primary purpose is love and pleasure, which are always reliable and faithful to their mission. Right after he is ejected from his father's brain [as a sperm], Providence supplies him with a safe place, protected from any harm, within [lit. among the beddings] in his mother's womb, in [such] a way that no stranger can touch him. There Providence sustains him with his daily bread each and every day, according to his size, and also deals with all his needs, not forgetting him for a minute, until he has enough strength to come out into the air of our obstacle-ridden world.

(11-7) Then Providence lends him strength and power, and like an old armed and experienced veteran hero, he moves ahead and opens gates and shatters his walls until he comes upon such people

המכתב, אשר בהכרח שיש מציאות של עיקר חוץ מהחותם, אמנם חוץ מגבול האמת, ודאי שאין שם מציאות כלל. ה', היתכן למלאכי אמת, לחשוב לפועל אמת, שאין ח"ו חס ושלום פעולתו אמת. ו', מה הגיע לו להאמת מתוך עונשו הקשה שנשלך עד לארץ ולתוך הארץ. ז', למה לא מובא תשובת המלאכים בתורה כמו שמובא השאלה אליהם.

## ההשגחה השולטת במציאות

(יא-5) וצריך להבין אותם ב' ההנהגות הערוכות לעינינו, ההפכים מן הקצה אל הקצה הנהגה שהם הווית כל המציאות של עולם הזה, והנהגה של אופני הקיום, להעמדתם של כאו"א כל אחד ואחד, מהמציאות שלפנינו. כי מקצה מזה, אנו מוצאים ההנהגה נאמנה, בהשגחה מאושרה עד להפליא, השולטת, להתהוות כל בריה ובריה מהמציאות, וניקח לדוגמא, סדרי הויה למציאות האדם.

(יא-6) והנה האהבה והעונג סבה ראשונה שלו, הבטוחה והנאמנה לשליחותה, ותיכף אחר שנעקר ממוח אביו, ההשגחה מזמנת לו מקום בטוח, משומר מכל נזק, בין המצעות שבבטן אמו, באופן שכל זר לא יגע בו, שמה, ההשגחה מכלכלת לו לחם חוקו, דבר יום ביומו, לפי מדתו, וכן מטפלת עמו בכל צרכיו, לא תשכחהו רגע, עד שירכוש לו חיל, לצאת לאויר ארצינו המלאה מעקשים.

(יא-7) ואז, ההשגחה משאלת לו עצמה וכח, וכמו גבור מזויין זקן ורגיל, הולך ופותח שערים ושובר בחומותיו. עד שבא בין אנשים כאלו, שאפשר לבטח עליהם, שיעזרוהו כל ימי חולשתו, להיותם

who can be trusted and who will help him with love and mercy and immense longing to sustain his very existence throughout his infancy [lit. the days of his weakness] because they are the dearest to him of all the people in the world. And so Providence proceeds to embrace him until it makes him fit for his existence and for the perpetuation of his existence after him. And just as with humans, this is also the case with animals and plants. They are all under supervision, with great wonder which secures their very existence, and all the scientists know this.

## The Illusion of No Providence

(11-8) On the other hand, when we look at the orders of the positioning and the economy of the modes of existence of those realities "from the horns of rams to the eggs of lice," (Tractate Shabbat 107b) we find confusion of order, just like in a camp of an army that runs away from the battlefield, beaten and sick and afflicted by the Creator. And all their vigor is for killing, for they have no way of existence, except through going through pain and suffering first. They earn their bread at great danger. Even the smallest louse breaks its teeth when going out to find food, and how much moaning it moans until it gets enough food to eat according to its needs so that it can exist. And this situation is similar to all [beings], from the smallest to the biggest, [even,] needless to say, the human species— the selected among all creatures—that has "his hand against every man and every man's hand against him." (Genesis 16:12).

היקרים לו מכל בני חלד, באהבה ורחמים וגעגועים עצומים בעד קיום מציאותו, וכן הולכת ההשגחה ומחבקתו עד שמכשרתו למציאותו ולהשתלשלות מציאותו אחריו. וכמקרה האדם כן מקרה מין החי, ומין הצומח, כולם מושגחים בהפלאה יתירה המבטחת הויתם למציאותם, וידעו זאת כל חכמי הטבע.

## אשליית חוסר ההשגחה

(יא-8) ומעבר מזה מקצה השני, בהסכלותינו על סדרי העמדה וכלכלה באופני הקיום של אותם המציאות מקרני ראמים עד ביצי כינים (מסכת שבת קז ע״ב), **אנו מוצאים בלבול סדרים**, כמו בין מחנה הבורחת משדה המערכה מוכים וחולים נגועי אלהי״ם, וכל חיתם לממותים, אין להם זכות קיום, זולת בהקדם יסורין ומכאובים, ובנפשם יביאו לחמם, ואפי' ואפילו כנה הקטנה שוברת שניה בעת צאתה לסעודתה, וכמה כרכורים היא מכרכרת עד שמשגת אוכל לפיה די סעודתה, לזכות קיומה, וכמוה מקרה אחד לכולם הקטנים עם הגדולים, ואינו צריך לומר במין האדם מובחר היצורים אשר ידו בכל ויד כל בו (בראשית טז, יב).

# Chapter 12: The Pattern of Creation (A)

## Inner Light and Surrounding Light

(12-1) Even in the Ten *Sefirot* of Holiness, we can discern the significance of two opposites, with the first nine *Sefirot* being all about sharing and the *Sefira* of *Malchut* (Kingdom) being all about receiving. Moreover, the first nine *Sefirot* are full of Light, while *Malchut* has nothing and generates nothing on its own. This is the secret of what we notice in every *Partzuf* (Spiritual Structure), two kinds of Light, which are categorized as Inner Light and Surrounding Light, as well as two kinds of Vessels, which are the Inner Vessel for the Inner Light and an External Vessel for the Surrounding Light.

(12-2) This [separation exists] because of the above-mentioned two opposites, since it is not possible for two opposites to come together in one object. Therefore, it is required that there be a special retaining object for the Inner Light and another retaining object for the Surrounding Light, as I have explained at length in the book *Panim Meirot Umasbirot* (*Enlightening and Explaining Face*), branches B and D.

## One and Its Opposite

(12-3) Yet, in the [Reality of] Holiness, they are not really opposites because [the *Sefira* of] *Malchut* is united together with the first nine *Sefirot* in the secret of [spiritual] unification. Thus, [*Malchut*'s] quality is also to share, according to the secret of Returning Light, as is discussed in *Panim Meirot Umasbirot* (*Enlightening and Explaining Face*), branch D. This, however, is not the case with [the Reality of] the *Sitra Achra* (the Other Side or Impurity), which has nothing of the first nine *Sefirot* in it. All its structure is out of the Vacant Space, which has to do with the magnitude of the Form of the [Desire to] Receive, upon which the first *Tzimtzum* (Contraction) took place.

# פרק יב: תבנית הבריאה (א)

## אור פנימי ואור מקיף

(יב-1) אמנם גם בעשר ספירות דקדושה, אנו מבחינים, ערך של ב' הפכים, להיות ט' ספירות ראשונות ענינם בצורת השפעה, ומלכות ענינה לקבלה, וכן ט"ר ט' (ספירות) ראשונות מלאים אור, והמלכות, לית לה מגרמה ולא מידי אין לה משל עצמה ולא כלום, וז"ס וזה סוד שאנו מבחינים בכל פרצוף, ב' בחי' בחינות באור, שהם או"פ אור פנימי ואו"מ ואור מקיף, וב' בחי' בחינות בכלים, שהם כלי פנימי לאו"פ אור פנימי וכלי חיצון לאור מקיף.

(יב-2) והוא מסבת ב' הפכים הנז' (הנזכרים) שא"א שאי אפשר לב' הפכים שיבואו בנושא אחד, וע"כ ועל כן צריכים לנושא מיוחד, לאו"פ לאור פנימי, ולנושא מיוחד לאור מקיף, כמו שהארכתי בפמ"ס בפנים מסבירות ענף ב' וד'.

## זה לעומת זה

(יב-3) אולם בקדושה אינם הפכים ממש, להיות המלכות נמצאת עם הט"ר ט' [ספירות] ראשונות בסוד הזיווג, ויהי' יהיה גם תכונתה להשפיע בסוד או"ח אור חוזר, כמ"ש כמו שנאמר בפמ"ס בפנים מסבירות ענף ד'. משא"כ מה שאין כן הס"א הסטרא אחרא, (הצד האחר) שאין להם מבחי' מבחינת ט"ר ט' ראשונות כלום ועיקר בנינם מחלל הפנוי שהוא ענין גדלות הצורה של קבלה, שעליה הי' היה הצמצום הא'.

(12-4) And even after the Illumination of the Line reached the *reshimu* (impression), this root remained without Light, as is discussed in the *Panim Meirot Umasbirot*, branch A. And therefore, it [the *Sitra Achra*] is the complete opposite from head to foot to life and to the Holiness. [And] this is the secret meaning of the passage: "The Creator made the one as well as the other." (Ecclesiastes 7:14) And therefore, they are called dead, as is stated there.

## *Katnut* (Being Small) and *Gadlut* (Being Adult)

(12-5) We have explained above in verse 6 that the whole purpose of the *Tzimtzum* (Contraction) was so that the souls could be adorned by Similarity of Form with their Maker, which is the transformation of the Vessels of Receiving into the Form of Sharing, as is discussed there (6-8). And in that state, it is found that this goal is still negated by the construction of the *Partzufim* (Spiritual Structures) of [the Reality of] Holiness because there is no existence there for the Vacant Space, which is the Form of the magnitude of the [Desire to] Receive, on which the *Tzimtzum* (Contraction) was applied, and therefore, there can be no Correction to something that is not in reality there. Similarly, from the aspect of the construction of the *Sitra Achra* (Other Side), there is surely no Correction, even though they have the aspect of the Vacant Space, because the [Other Side] is completely the opposite [to Holiness] and everything that it receives is destined for death.

(12-6) Therefore, a man of This World is what we need. In his *katnut* (smallness), he is found to be sustained and fed by the *Sitra Achra* (Other Side), and he inherits from it the Vessels of the Vacant Space. But in his *gadlut* (maturity), he crosses over and becomes connected to the structure of Holiness by virtue of the Torah and the Precepts through giving pleasure to his Maker. And thus he transforms the magnitude of the [Desire to] Receive that he has already acquired so that it is arranged in him only for the Sake of Sharing. In this, he is found to be making his Form similar to that of the Creator, and thus the intention [of the Creator] is fulfilled in [this person].

(יב-4) שאפי' אפילו אחר שהגיע הארת הקו לוך הרשימו נשאר שורש הזה בלי אור כמש"כ כמו שכתוב בפמ"ס בפנים מסבירות **ענף א'** וע"כ ועל כן המה הפכים מראש עד רגל לעומת החיים והקדושה, בסוה"כ בסוד הכתוב זה לעומת זה עשה אלהי"ם (קוהלת ז', יד'), וע"כ ועל כן נקראים מתים כמ"ש כמו שכתוב שם.

## קטנות וגדלות

(יב-5) והנה נתבאר לעיל באות ו', שכל ענין הצמצום הי' רק להתקשטות הנשמות בדבר השוואת הצורה ליוצרם, שהוא ענין התהפכות כלי קבלה על צורת השפעה, כמו"ש כמו שנאמר שם (ו-8), ובמצב הנז' הנזכר, נמצא המטרה הזאת עודנה משוללת, הן מצד בנין פרצופין דקדושה, שאין שם כלום מבחי' מבחינת **חלל הפנוי**, שהוא צורת גדלות הקבלה, שעליה הי' היה הצמצום, וע"כ ועל כן, לא יארע שום תיקון לדבר שאינה שם במציאות, וכן מצד בנין הס"א הסטרא אחרא, (הצד האחר), ודאי אין כאן שום תיקון, אע"ג אף על גב שיש להם מבחי' מבחינת **חלל הפנוי**, שהרי ענינה הפוכה לגמרי, וכל מה שמקבלת למיתה עומד.

(יב-6) וע"כ ועל כן, אך לאדם דעולם הזה צריכין, שבקטנותו מצוי בכלכלה וקיום הס"א הסטרא אחרא, (הצד האחר), ויורש מהם הכלים דחלל הפנוי, ובגדולתו עובר ומתחבר לבנין הקדושה, בסגולת תורה ומצוות להשפיע נ"ר נחת רוח ליוצרו, ונמצא מהפך גדלות הקבלה שכבר קנה, שתהי' תהיה מסודרת בו רק ע"מ על מנת להשפיע, שנמצא בזה משוה הצורה ליוצרה, ומתקיים בו הכונה.

(12-7) And this is the secret of the existence of time in this world, because you find that from the beginning [that] these two opposites were divided into two realities [lit. subjects] separated from each other, namely the [Reality of] Holiness and [the Reality of] the *Sitra Achra* (Other Side), according to the secret of "one is the opposite of the other." This is because the Correction was still withheld from them, as mentioned above (12-5), since [both opposites] have to be present in the same retaining object, which is man, as mentioned above (12-6). And therefore, we must have, of necessity, a [linear] order of times because then the two opposites could appear in man, one after the other, that is, during the time of *katnut* (smallness) and the time of *gadlut* (maturity), as was said before (ibid).

(יב-7) וזה סוד מציאת הזמן בעולם הזה, דהנך מוצא שמתחילה נתחלקו ב' ההפכים הנ"ל, לב' נושאים נפרדים זה מזה, דהיינו הקדושה, והס"א והסטרא אחרא, (הצד האחר), בסוד זה לעומת זה, שעדיין נשלל מהם התיקון כנ"ל (יב-5), מפני שמחוייבים להמצא בנושא אחד, שהוא האדם, כנ"ל (יב-6). וע"כ ועל כן בהכרח, למציאות סדר זמנים אנו צריכים, שאז יהי' ב' ההפכים באים בהאדם, בזה אחר זה, כלומר, בזמן קטנות, ובזמן גדלות כאמור (יב-6).

# Chapter 13: The Pattern of Creation (B)

## Direct Light and Returning Light

(13-1) Through this, you will understand the need for the Shattering of the Vessels and their qualities, as is discussed in the *Zohar* and in the *Writings* of the Ari, Rav Isaac Luria. For it is known that there are two kinds of Light that can be found going back and forth (Heb. *ratzo vashov*) throughout the Ten *Sefirot*. The first Light is the Light of *Ein Sof* (Endless), which goes "forth" from Above downwards and is called *Or Yashar* (Straight or Direct Light). The second Light, which is generated by the Vessel of *Malchut* (Kingdom), goes "back" from Below upwards and is called *Or Chozer* (Returning Light). These two [forms of Light] actually unite into one [Light].

(13-2) And you should know what [the sages] said: That from the *tzimtzum* (contraction) downwards, the point of *tzimtzum* is prevented from receiving any Light at all and remains a Vacant Space, and that the Supernal Light no longer appears in the last [fourth] phase before the Correction is completed. All this has been said particularly with regard to the Endless Light, which is called Direct Light. But the second Light, which is called Returning Light, can appear in the last [Fourth] Phase because the *Tzimtzum* does not apply to [the second Light] at all.

(13-3) Thus it has been explained that the System of the *Sitra Achra* (Other Side) and the *klippot (shells)* is necessary for the purpose of the *Tzimtzum* (Contraction) in order to instill in man the Vessels of the magnitude of the [Desire to] Receive during the time of his *katnut* (smallness) while he is still being nourished by them. But the *Sitra Achra* also needs sustenance, and where will it take it from, being that all its construction is only from the last phase, which is the Vacant Space that is void of any Light? This is because from the *Tzimtzum* (Contraction) downwards, the Supernal Light is completely separate from there.

# פרק יג: תבנית הבריאה (ב)

## אור ישר ואור חוזר

(יג-1) ובזה תבין הצורך לשבירת הכלים ותכונתם כמ"ש כמו שכתוב בזהר וכהאר"י וכתבי האר"י, דנודע, דב' מיני אור נמצאים בכל ע"ס עשר ספירות: ברצוא ושוב. אור הא', הוא אור אין סוף ב"ה ברוך הוא, הרצוא מלמעלה למטה, ונקרא אור ישר. ואור הב', הוא תולדות כלי המלכות, השוב מלמטה למעלה, ונק' אור חוזר. אשר שניהם מתחברים לאחד ממש.

(יג-2) ותדע, דהא דאמרינן שכך אמרו [המקובלים], אשר מהצמצום ולמטה, כבר נשללת נקודת הצמצום מכל אור, ונשארה חלל פנוי, ואור העליון לא יופיע עוד לבחי' בחינה אחרונה, בטרם גמר התיקון שזה נאמר ביחוד, על אור א"ס ב"ה אין סוף ברוך הוא, שנקרא אור ישר, אבל אור הב', הנקרא אור חוזר, הוא יכול להופיע לבחי' לבחינה אחרונה, היות, שעליו לא הי' היה מקרה הצמצום כלל.

(יג-3) ונתבאר אשר מערכת הס"א הסטרא אחרא (הצד האחר) והקלי' והקליפה, הוא צורך מחוייב, למטרתה של הצמצום, והוא, כדי להטביע בהאדם כלי גדלות הקבלה, בעת קטנותו, בהיותו סמוך על שולחנה, וא"כ ואם כן הרי הס"א הסטרא אחרא ג"כ גם כן, לשפע היא צריכה, ומאין תקח זה, בהיות כל בנינה רק מבחי' מבחינה אחרונה, שהוא חלל פנוי מכל אור, אשר מהצמצום ולמטה, כבר אור העליון נפרד משם לגמרי.

## Pure and Impure Realities

(13-4) And therefore the Shattering of the Vessels was prepared. The Shattering signifies the separate part of the Returning Light in the Ten *Sefirot* of the World of *Nekudim* (dots), which descended from [the World of] *Atzilut* (Emanation) outwards, [down] into the Vacant Space. You already know that the Returning Light can appear also in the Vacant Space. And so this part of the Returning Light, which descended from [the World of] *Atzilut* outwards, contains within itself, from each and every one of the *Sefirot* of the Ten *Sefirot* of the [World of] *Nekudim*, *lev* (32) special aspects, as explained in its place; and 10 times *lev* (32) is *shach* (320).

(13-5) And these *shach* (320) aspects that descended were prepared for the sake of the existence of the Lower [physical realities], which appear as two systems. This is according to the secret [inner meaning] of the verse, "The Creator has made one as well as the other." (Ecclesiastes 7:14) In other words, there are the Worlds of *Atzilut* (Emanation), *Beriah* (Creation), *Yetzirah* (Formation), and *Asiyah* (Action) of Holiness, and opposite to them are the Worlds of *Atzilut*, *Beriah*, *Yetzirah*, and *Asiyah* of the *Sitra Achra* (Other Side).

(13-6) And this is what our sages said (Tractate *Megilah*, 6a) in interpreting the passage, "one nation shall be stronger than the other." (Genesis 25:23) When a certain [nation] rises, the other falls, [that is, the city of] Tzor only gets built by the destruction of Jerusalem, see there. This is because these *shach* (320) aspects may all appear in the *Sitra Achra* (Other Side), and then, Heaven forbid, the construction of the System of Holiness is destroyed completely with respect to the Lower [physical realities]. But it is possible that all these [320 aspects] connect to the [System of] Holiness, and then the System of the *Sitra Achra* is destroyed and is completely removed from the earth. It is also possible for [these 320 aspects] to be divided between the two [Systems], to a greater or a lesser degree, according to the action of human beings. And so [these 320 aspects] rotate between the two Systems until the Correction [process] is completed.

## עולמות קדושה ועולמות טומאה

(יג-4) ולפיכך הוכן ענין שביה"כ שבירת הכלים, שענין שבירה יורה, ענין הפרש חלק מאור חוזר, שבעשר ספירות דעולם הנקודים, שירד מאצילות ולחוץ, עד לחלל הפנוי, וכבר ידעת, שאור חוזר, אפשר לו להופיע גם לחלל הפנוי. והנה בזה החלק או"ח אור חוזר, שירד מאצילות ולחוץ, יש בו מכל ספירה וספירה, דע"ס דעשר ספירות דנקודים, ל"ב בחי' בחינות מיוחדות, כמו"ש כמו שכתוב במקומו, ועשרה פעמים ל"ב, הוא ש"ך.

(יג-5) וש"ך בחי' בחינות אלו שירדו, הוכנו, לקיום המציאות, של התחתונים, שהמה באים להם בב' מערכות, בסו"ה בסוד הכתוב זה לעומת זה עשה אלהי"ם (קוהלת ז',יד'), דהיינו עולמות אבי"ע אצילות, בריאה, יצירה, עשיה דקדושה, ולעומתם עולמות אבי"ע אצילות, בריאה, יצירה, עשיה דס"א של הסטרא אחרא, (הצד האחר).

(יג-6) והיינו שאמרו [חכמינו] ז"ל [במסכת] מגילה [דף] ו' ע"א עמוד א', בביאור הכתוב, ולאום מלאום יאמץ' (בראשית כה, כג), כי כשקם זה נופל זה, ולא נבנית צור אלא מחורבנה של ירושלם (רש"י בראשית כ"ה כ"ג). ש"ך הבחי' בחינות האלו, אפשר להם, שיופיעו כולם לס"א לסטרא אחרא, (הצד האחר), ואז נחרב ח"ו חס ושלום בנין מערכת הקדושה, כלפי התחתונים לגמרי. ואפשר להם, שיתחברו כולם לקדושה, ואז נמצא נחרבת מערכת הס"א הסטרא אחרא לגמרי מהארץ. ואפשר להם, שיתחלקו בין שתיהם, בפחות ויתר, לפי מעשי בני אדם. וכך הם מתגלגלים בב' המערכות, עד גומרו של התיקון.

## The Shattering of the Vessels

(13-7) After the Shattering of the Vessels and the descent of the above-mentioned *shach* (320) sparks of Light from [the World of] *Atzilut* (Emanation) outwards, the *rapach* (288) of the sparks were refined and they ascended. This refers to what [originally] descended from the first nine *Sefirot* of the Ten *Sefirot* of the [World of] *Nekudim* (dots), and 9 times *lev* (32) are *rapach* (288) sparks. And these [288 sparks] returned and joined the construction of the System of Holiness.

(13-8) So what was left to the *Sitra Achra* (Other Side) was only *lev* (32) sparks, referring to those which [originally] descended from the *Malchut* (Kingdom) of the World of *Nekudim*. [These 32 sparks] became the beginning of the construction of the *Sitra Achra*, albeit in a small measure, since it was not yet ready for its role. The completion of the construction happened later because of the sin of Adam with regard to the Tree of Knowledge [of Good and Evil], as is explained in [the book] *Tree of Life*.

(13-9) Hereby it has been clarified how the two Systems of "one as an opposite of the other" supervise the existence and the nourishment of reality. The amount of Light that is necessary for this existence is *shach* (320) sparks, which were prepared and measured by the power of the Shattering of the Vessels. This specified amount is destined to migrate between the two Systems [of Holiness and of the Other Side] because the order of existence and the sustenance of reality depend on it. And you should know that the System of Holiness must contain at least the specified amount of the *rapach* (288) sparks in order to complete its first nine *Sefirot*, as mentioned above (13-7), and then it is able to sustain and nourish the existence of the Lower [physical realities]. This was the case before the sin of Adam, and therefore, all of reality was supervised according to the System of Holiness at that time because it had the full amount of all the *rapach* (288) sparks, as explained (ibid).

## שבירת הכלים

(יג-7) **והנה** לאחר שביה"כ שבירת הכלים, וירידתם של ש"ך (320) בחי'
בחינות ניצוצי אורה הנ"ל, מאצילות ולחוץ, נתבררו ועלו מהם רפ"ח
(288) ניצוצין. דהיינו כל מה שירד מתשעה ספירות הראשונות,
שבע"ס שבעשר ספירות דנקודים, וט' פעמים ל"ב (32) הוא רפ"ח (288)
בחי' בחינות. והמה שבו ונתחברו, לבנין מערכת הקדושה.


(יג-8) **ונמצא** נשאר לס"א לסטרא אחרא, (הצד האחר), רק ל"ב (32) בחי'
בחינות, ממה שירד מהמלכות דעולם הנקודים. והי' היה זה, לתחילת
בנין הס"א הסטרא אחרא, במיעוט בתכלית, שעדיין איננה ראויה
לתפקידה, ומילוא בנינה נגמר להם אח"כ אחר כך, בסיבת חטאו של
אדם הראשון בעץ הדעת, כמ"ש כמו שכתוב בע"ה בעץ החיים.


(יג-9) **והנה** נתבאר שב' מערכות זה לעומת זה, נוהגת בקיום
ופרנסת המציאות. ותקציב אור הצריך לזה הקיום הוא ש"ך (320)
ניצוצין. והמה הוכנו ונמדדו, בכח שביה"כ שבירת הכלים. ותקציב
הזה ראוי להתגלגל, בין ב' המערכות אשר בזה תלוי סדרי הקיום
והכלכלה של המציאות. ותדע שמערכת הקדושה מחוייבת להכיל,
לכל הפחות תקציב של רפ"ח (288) ניצוצין להשלמת ט' ספירות
ראשונות שלה, כנ"ל (יג-7), ואז יכולה לקיים ולכלכל מציאות
התחתונים. וזה היה לה קודם חטאו של אה"ר אדם הראשון, וע"כ ועל
כן היה לה כל המציאות מתנהגת אז, ע"י על ידי מערכת הקדושה, להיות
שהיה לה המילוא של רפ"ח (288) ניצוצין כאמור (שם).

# *Chapter 14: Angels Arguing*

## Upside Down World

(14-1) So now we have found the opening from the *Midrash* to the passage above (11-1) regarding the four groups [of angels]—Mercy, Righteousness, Truth, and Peace—who were debating with the Creator about the creation of mankind. Because these angels are those who serve the soul of mankind (study, in [the book] *The Tree of Life*, the essays about the Worlds: Emanation, Creation, Formation and Action), therefore [the Creator] conferred with them because every act of creation was carried out according to their consent, as our sages have said (ibid). And it is known that each and every soul includes the essence of the Ten *Sefirot* with their Inner Light and Surrounding Light. Mercy is the essence of the Inner Light of the first nine *Sefirot* of the soul, and Righteousness is the essence of the Inner Light of the [*Sefira* of] *Malchut* (Kingdom) of the soul. Truth is the essence of the Surrounding Light of the soul.

(14-2) We have already mentioned that the Inner Light and the Surrounding Light are opposites. This is because the Inner Light is drawn by the law of the illumination of the Line, which was prevented from appearing at the point of *Tzimtzum* (Contraction), [this point being] the Form of the magnitude of the [Desire to] Receive, while the Surrounding Light is drawn from the Endless Light, which surrounds all the Worlds. And since in the Endless, small and large are equal, consequently the Surrounding Light shines and bestows goodness upon the point of *Tzimtzum* as well and even more so upon the aspect of *Malchut* (Kingdom).

(14-3) But since they [Inner Light and Surrounding Light] are opposites, therefore they need two Vessels. This is because the Inner Light illuminates the first nine [*Sefirot*], however, it illuminates *Malchut* (Kingdom) only by the directive of the first nine [*Sefirot*]

# פרק יד: הויכוח של המלאכים

## עולם הפוך

(יד-1) **ועתה** מצאנו הפתח, להמדרש הנ"ל (יא-1) בענין ד' הכתוב, חסד וצדקה אמת ושלום, שנשאו ונתנו עם השי"ת השם יתברך, בבריאת אדם. כי המלאכים הללו, המה משמשי הנשמה של האדם, (ועי' עיין בע"ח בעץ חיים ש' דרושי אבי"ע אצילות, בריאה, יצירה, עשיה) ולכן נשא ונתן עמהם, להיות כל מעשה בראשית לדעתם נבראו, כאמרם ז"ל (שם). ונודע, שכל נשמה ונשמה כוללת ענין, ע"ס עשר ספירות, באו"פ באור פנימי ואו"מ ואור מקיף, והנה החסד, הוא ענין או"פ אור פנימי של ט"ר ט' ראשונות של הנשמה. והצדקה, ה"ע הוא עניין או"פ אור פנימי של המלכות של הנשמה.

(יד-2) **וכבר** דברנו שאו"פ שאור פנימי ואו"מ ואור מקיף הפכים המה. להיות האו"פ האור פנימי נמשך בחוק הארת הקו, שנמנע מלהופיע לנקודת הצמצום, שהיא צורת הגדלות של הקבלה. ואו"מ ואור מקיף נמשך מאור א"ס אין סוף ב"ה ברוך הוא, המקיף לכל העולמות, ששם בא"ס באין סוף שוה קטן וגדול וע"כ ועל כן או"מ אור מקיף מאיר ומטיב לנקודת הצמצום ג"כ גם כן, ומכ"ש ומכל שכן לבחי' לבחינת המלכות.

(יד-3) **וכיון** שהמה הפכים, א"כ אם כן לב' כלים צריכים, כי או"פ אור פנימי מאיר בט"ר בט' [ספירות] ראשונות, וכן אפי' אפילו למלכות אינו מאיר אלא בחוק ט"ר ט' [ספירות] ראשונות, ולא כלל לבחינתה עצמה. אמנם

and not at all in its own aspect. The Surrounding Light, however, illuminates specifically the Vessels that extend from the point of *Tzimtzum* (Contraction), which is called External Vessel.

## True Seal

(14-4) This will make you understand why Truth was called a seal. It is because this name is borrowed from the seal that appears at the bottom of a letter at the end of the discussed issues. And indeed, [the seal] validates them and gives them credibility because without the seal, the words [would] have no value and the whole letter would be worthless. And so it is [also] with the Surrounding Light that bestows goodness upon the point of *Tzimtzum* (Contraction), which is the idea of the magnitude of the [Desire to] Receive, until [the aspect of receiving] makes its Form similar to that of its Maker—that is, the aspect of sharing, as was explained above (11-6)—this being the purpose of all the limited Worlds: The Upper and the Lower.

(14-5) So the protest of [the Angel of] Truth regarding the creation of man—[Truth's] claim that human beings would be all lies—was because from the aspect of the action of the Creator, [man] had no external Vessel, which he would need to draw from the point of *tzimtzum* (contraction), since [the point] had already separated itself from [the Creator's] Light, as was said above (13-3). Therefore, the Angels of Truth could not help mankind in obtaining the Surrounding Light. And thus, all the limited Worlds, Upper and Lower—which had been created solely for this completion and man, is required to be the sole objective of this [completion], yet he was not adequately fit for his purpose—are therefore all chaos and a lie, and all the labor in them is of no avail.

(14-6) However, the Angels of Mercy and Righteousness, which belong in particular to the Inner Light of the soul, could then bestow upon them [humans] all the lights of the soul to a great extent,

או"מ אור מקיף, מאיר בכלים הנמשכים מנקודת הצמצום ביחוד, שנק' שנקרא כלי חיצון.

## חותם אמת

(יד-4) ובזה תבין, למה נקרא האמת חותם, כי שם זה, מושאל, מחותם הבא בשולי המכתב בסוף העניינים, אמנם הוא מעמידם ומקיימם, כי זולת החותם, אין בהם שום ערך, וכל הכתב הוי לבטלה. וכן ענין או"מ אור מקיף המטיב לנקודת הצמצום, שה"ע הוא עניין גדלות הקבלה, עד שמשוה צורתה ליוצרה בבחי' בבחינת השפעה כנ"ל (11-ו), שהיא מטרת כל העולמות עליונים ותחתונים המוגבלים.

(יד-5) **והיינו** המחאה של האמת, בבריאת האדם, כי טען שכולו שקרים, להיות שמצד יצירתו של הקב"ה הקדוש ברוך הוא, אין להאדם כלי חיצון, שהוא צריך להמשך מנקודת הצמצום בשכבר נפרדה מאורו ית' כאמור לעיל (יג-3). וא"כ ואם כן, אי אפשר למלאכי אמת, להועיל להאדם בהשגת אור מקיף, וא"כ ואם כן כל העולמות העליונים והתחתונים המוגבלים, שלא נבראו אלא להשלמה הזו, ואשר זה האדם צריך להיות הנושא היחיד אליה, וכיון שהאדם הזה אינו מוכשר למטרתו. א"כ אם כן כולם המה תוהו ושקר, וכל הטרחא בהם ללא הועיל.

(יד-6) אמנם מלאכי חסד וצדקה, שהמה שייכים ביחוד, לאו"פ לאור פנימי של הנשמה, אדרבא משום זה שאין לו כלל מבחי' בחינת חלל הפנוי, היו יכולים להשפיע לו כל אורות הנשמה בהרוחה יתירה,

even to the utmost perfection, because [humans] have nothing from the aspect of the Vacant Space. Therefore, [the Angels] were happy to benefit them and wholeheartedly agreed to the creation of mankind. The Angels of Peace claimed that humans would be all quarrels, in other words, how [were] they going to receive the Surrounding Light [when,] after all, it would be impossible for [humanity] to be joined as one matter with the Inner Light, being that both are opposites of each other, as was explained? And this is why [mankind] is all quarrels.

על השלימות היותר נעלה, ולפיכך היו שמחים להועילו, והסכימו בכל מאדם על בריאת האדם. ומלאכי השלום, טענו דכולו קטטה, כלומר, איך שיהיה ענין קבלתו את האו"מ האור מקיף, אמנם סוף סוף אי אפשר שיבואו בנושא אחד עם האו"פ האור הפנימי, להיותם הפוכים זל"ז זה לזה, כאמור, והיינו כולו קטטה.

# Chapter 15: The Tree of Knowledge Good and Evil

## Lack and Need Create Shame

(15-1) By what has been said [here], we have merited an understanding of the continuation of the verses [in Genesis] regarding the sin of the Tree of Knowledge of Good and Evil. [These verses] have unfathomable depth, and our sages have unveiled [just] one layer [lit. handbreadth] of their meaning while [on the other hand] covering ten. We find at the beginning of the text that it is written: "And the Man (Adam) and his wife were both naked, and were not ashamed." (Genesis 2:25) You should know [here] that clothing refers to the External Vessel, as was said in *Etz Chaim* (*The Tree of Life*) in the chapters on [the Worlds of] *Atzilut* (Emanation), *Beriah* (Creation), *Yetzirah* (Formation), and *Asiyah* (Action); study there.

(15-2) And therefore, the Scripture tells us in advance to teach us the reason for the sin of the Tree of Knowledge, as our sages said regarding the verse: "He is fearful in his defaming of the descendants of Adam," (Psalms 66:5) where [mankind] was framed, meaning that the sin was prepared for him in advance. This is what the text means, that Adam and his wife were from the side of [the World of] *Yetzirah* (Formation), with no External Vessel, only with Inner Vessels, which are extended from the System of Holiness, as was discussed above (15-1). And therefore, they were not ashamed, that is, they did not feel their emptiness because shame is, in fact, a
 feeling of lack and need.

(15-3) It is known that the feeling of lack is the first reason to fulfill that lack. It is like a person who feels sick [and] is then ready to receive medication, while he who does not feel he is sick surely avoids any kind of medicine. Indeed, this role is assigned to the External Vessel, which, being part of the construction of the body,

# פרק טו: עץ הדעת טוב ורע

## החסרון גורם בושה

(טו-1) ובהאמור, זכינו להבין המשך הפסוקים, בחטאו של עץ הדעת טוב ורע, אשר עומק רום להם, וחז"ל שגילו בהם טפח, עוד כסו בדבריהם עשרה טפחים. והנה בהקדם העניין כתיב, ויהיו האדם ואשתו שניהם ערומים ולא יתבוששו (בראשית ב, כה). ודע, שעניין לבוש, ה"א עניין כלי חיצון, כמ"ש כמו שכתוב בע"ח [של האר"י] ב[ספר] עץ חיים שער דרושי אבי"ע אצילות, בריאה, יצירה, עשיה, ע"ש עיין שם, .....

(טו-2) וע"כ ועל כן מקדים לנו הכתוב, להורות סיבת חטאו של עצה"ד עץ הדעת, ע"ד על דרך שאמרו ז"ל, בהפסוק נורא עלילה לבני אדם (תהילים סו, ה), אשר בעלילה באת עלי עליו. כלומר, שהי' היה מוכן לו חטאו מכל מראש. וזה שיעור הכתוב, שהיו האדם ואשתו מצד היצירה, בלי כלי חיצון, רק בבחינת כלים פנימים, הנמשכים ממערכת הקדושה כנ"ל (טו-1), וע"כ ועל כן ולא יתבוששו, כלומר, שלא הרגישו בחסרונם, כי הבושה ה"א עניין הרגשת חסרון.

(טו-3) ונודע, שהרגשת החסרון, הוא סיבה ראשונה למלאות החסרון בדומה, להמרגיש בחליו, מוכן הוא לקבל רפואה, אבל האינו מרגיש כי חולה הוא, נמצא נמנע בודאי מכל רפואה. אכן תפקיד הזה מוטל הוא על כלי חיצונה, שבהיותה בבניין הגוף, והיא

is empty of Light because it [the empty Vessel] came from the Vacant Space, [and] it therefore arouses in [a person] the feeling of emptiness and of lack, so he is ashamed of it.

(15-4) For this reason, he must go back and fulfill that lack and draw the Surrounding Light he is missing so that it can fill this Vessel. And this is the meaning of the text: "and the Man (Adam) and his wife were both naked" (Genesis 2:25); that is, they did not have an External Vessel, and therefore, they were not ashamed because they did not feel their lack. Therefore, they were deprived of [fulfilling] the goal for which they had been created.

*[handwritten margin note: God's reason 4 creating man]*

## The Sin of Adam

(15-5) Indeed, we need to understand deeply the high *komah* (stature) of this human being, who was the product of the Creator, and [the high *komah*] of his wife, who was granted by the Creator an additional intelligence (*binah*), as the sages said (in Tractate *Niddah*, 45) in explaining the meaning of the passage: "and the Creator constructed (Heb. *Vayiven* = construct and also understand) from the rib..." (Genesis 2:22) So how did they [Adam and Eve] fail and become like fools, not knowing to take precautions against the craftiness of the Serpent?

(15-6) On the other hand, how could the Serpent, which the Bible says was subtler than any of the other wild creatures, utter such recklessness and foolishness, [telling them] that if they ate the fruit of the Tree of Knowledge, then they would become [like the] Creator [lit. *Elohim*]? How did such folly find a nest in their hearts? Furthermore, it is said later on that it was not because of the desire to become [the] Creator that she ate from the Tree of Knowledge, but simply because "the tree was tasty for eating, etc.," (Genesis 3:6) which is, on the face of it, a beastly desire.

ריקנית מאור, מסבת שבאה מחלל הפנוי נמצאת מולידה בו, הרגש הריקנות והחסרון, ומתבייש מזה.

(טו-4) וע"כ ועל כן מוכרח, שיחזור למלאות החסרון, ולהמשיך האו"מ האור מקיף החסר לו, שהוא עומד למלאות את כלי הזו. וזהו הוראת הכתוב, ויהי' ויהיו האדם ואשתו שניהם ערומים (בראשית ב, כה), מכלי חיצון, ולפיכך ולא יתבוששו, שלא הרגישו חסרונם, ונמצאים משוללים מהמטרה שעליה נבראו.

## חטא אדם וחוה

(טו-5) אמנם צריך להבין מאד, רוממות זה האדם יציר כפיו של הקב"ה הקדוש ברוך הוא, ואשתו שהקב"ה שהקדוש ברוך הוא חלק לה עוד בינה יתירה הימנו, כאמרם ז"ל [מסכת] נדה עמוד מ"ה) בהבנת הכתוב ויבן ה' את הצלע (בראשית ב, כב), ואיככה נכשלו ונעשו ככסילים, לא ידעו להזהר מערמת הנחש.

(טו-6) גם לאידך גיסא, זה הנחש, שהמקרא מעיד עליו, שהיה ערום מכל חית השדה, איך הוציא משפתיו כסילות וריקות כזו, שבאם יאכלו לפרי העץ"ד העץ הדעת, אז יתהוה מהם אלהי"ם. ואיך כסילות זה מצא קן בלבבם. ועוד, כי להלן נאמר, שלא מפני התאוה להעשות אלהי"ם אכלה מעצה"ד מעץ הדעת, אלא בפשיטות, כי טוב העץ למאכל וכו' (בראשית ג, ו), שהוא לכאורה, תאוה בהמית.

## Chapter 16: The Ability to Discern

### Good and Evil, True and False

(16-1) We should know the nature of the two types of discernmentt that apply to us. The first type of discernment is called discerning between good and bad, while the second type of discernment is called discerning between truth and falsehood. That is to say, the Creator instilled the force of discerning in every living being, in whom it activates all the desired benefit, leading it into the desired perfection. The first [type of] discerning is a force that acts physically, and its operating system is through the sensing of bitter and sweet. [That force] despises and rejects that which is bitter because it feels bad, while [that force] delights and attracts sweetness because it feels good.

(16-2) This [first] acting force is sufficient in the Inanimate, Vegetative, and Animal species because it leads them to the completion of their desired perfection. Added to them is the Speaking species (that is, mankind), in whom the Creator instilled a mental acting force whose form of action is [part of] the second discerning process, in that it rejects falsehood and emptiness with disgust bordering on throwing up; instead, it attracts truthfulness and every benefit with great love.

(16-3) This [second type of] discerning is called discerning between truth and falsehood, and it applies only to mankind [and] in each person according to his level. And you should know that this second acting force was created and bestowed upon mankind because of the Serpent, because from the aspect of Creation, mankind would have only had the first acting force, the one that selects between good and evil, which would have been enough and sufficient for his needs and benefit at that time.

# פרק טז: היכולת להבחין

## טוב ורע, אמת ושקר

(טז-1) **וצריכים** לדעת, טיב של ב' מיני הבירורים הנוהגים אצלנו. בירור הא', נק' נקרא בירורי טוב ורע, בירור הב', נק' נקרא בירורי אמת ושקר. פי' פירוש, שהשי"ת שהשם יתברך הטביע כח המברר בכל בריה, שפועל בה כל התועלת הנרצה, ומעמידה על שלימותה הנרצה, והנה בירור הא' הוא כח הפועל גופני, שאופני פעולתו, ע"י על ידי הרגש מר ומתוק, שהוא ממאס ודוחה צורת המר, כי רע לו, ונאהב לו, ומקרב צורת המתוק, כי טוב לו.

(טז-2) והנה כח הפועל הזה, די ומספיק, בדוממ, צומח, וחי, שבהמציאות, שמעמידם על גמר שלימותם הנרצה. ונוסף עליהם מין האדם, שהטביע בו השי"ת השם יתברך כח פועל שכלי, שאופני פעולתו בבירור הב' הנ"ל, שדוחה עניני שקר וריקות, במיאוס עד להקאה, ומקרב ענינים אמיתיים, וכל תועלת, באהבה גדולה.

(טז-3) ובירור הזה, נק' נקרא בירור אמת ושקר ואינו נוהג זולת במין האדם כאו"א כל אחד ואחד לפי שיעורו. ותדע, שכח הפועל הזה הב', נברא והגיע להאדם, בסבת עטיו של הנחש, כי מצד היצירה, לא היה לו זולת כח הפועל הא', מבירורי טו"ר טוב ורע, שהיה די ומספיק לו לתועלתו בעת ההיא.

## Bitter and Sweet

(16-4) I will explain [this] to you by way of an example. Had the righteous been rewarded in accordance with their good deeds and the evil ones punished according to their evil actions in this World, then the [System of] Holiness would have been defined for us as a reality of the sweet and the good, and the [System of the] *Sitra Achra* (Other Side) would have been defined for us as the reality of the bitter and the evil. And this way, the Precept of free will [choice] would come to us by way of an injunction: "Behold, I have put before you the sweet and the bitter, and you shall choose the sweet." (According to Deuteronomy 30:19) In this manner, all people would have been sure of attaining perfection because surely they would have run away from sin since it would have been harmful to them. And they would have been busy with the Creator's Precepts day and night without any rest, and would not have been busy with the body and its impurities, as fools are at the present time, because [following the Creator's Precepts] would have been good and sweet for them.

(16-5) This was the case with Adam, the First Man, because when the Creator created him, He put him in the Garden of Eden "to work for it and to preserve (protect) it." (Genesis 2:15) [The sages] explained (*Zohar Beresheet*, 260) that the words "work for it" refer to the "do" Precepts, and [the words] "to preserve (protect) it" refer to the "do not" Precepts. [Adam's] "do" Precepts were to eat from and enjoy all the trees of the garden, his "do not" Precepts were to not eat from the Tree of Knowledge of Good and Evil. Thus, the "do" Precepts were sweet and pleasant, while the "do not" Precepts were to refrain from eating the fruit that was bitter and harsh as death.

(16-6) One should not wonder how [Adam's work] could be called Precepts and "work" because we have similarly found, even in the [spiritual] work that we do in the present, that by delighting in the *Shabbat* (Saturday) and the holidays, we gain the Sublime Holiness. Moreover, by refraining from eating insects and reptiles and

## מר ומתוק

(טז-4) ואסביר לך עד"מ על דרך משל, אם היו הצדיקים נגמלים כמפעלם הטוב, והרשעים נענשים על מעשיהם, כדי רשעתם, בעוה"ז בעולם הזה, היה אז הקדושה מוגדרת לנו, במציאות של המתוק והטוב. והס"א והסטרא אחרא, (הצד האחר) היתה מוגדרת לנו, במציאות של הרע והמר. ובאופן זה, היה מצוות הבחירה מגיענו, ע"ד על דרך ראה נתתי לפניך את המתוק ואת המר, ובחרת בהמתוק. ובאופן זה, היו כל בני אדם בטוחים בהשגת השלימות, שבטח היו בורחים מן העבירה, להיותה רע להם, והיו טרודים במצוותיו ית' יום ולילה לא יחשו, כמו הטפשים של עתה בעניני הגוף וזוהמתו, להיותה טוב ומתוק להם.

(טז-5) והנה כן היה ענין אדה"ר אדם הראשון, מפאת יצירתו ית' יתברך אותו. והניחוהו בג"ע בגן עדן, לעבדה ולשמרה (בראשית ב, טו), שפירשו חכמינו ז"ל (זוהר הסולם, בראשית, סעיף רס'): לעבדה אלו מצות עשה, ולשמרה אלו מצות לא תעשה, ומצות עשה שלו, היה לאכול ולהתענג מכל עצי הגן, ומצוות ל"ת לא תעשה שלו, היה שלא לאכול מעצה"ד מעץ הדעת טו"ר טוב ורע. אשר המצוות עשה, היתה מתוקה, ונחמדה, והמצות לא תעשה, היה הפרישה מן הפרי המר והקשה כמות.

(טז-6) ואין לתמוה איך אפשר להקרא כאלה, בשם מצוות ועבודה, כי מצינו כזה, גם בעבודתינו של עתה, אשר ע"י על ידי התענוג בשבתות ויו"ט ויום טוב, אנו זוכים לקדושה העליונה, וכן על ידי

everything else that is despicable to mankind's *Nefesh* (Lower Soul), we receive rewards. And we find that [this] choice [that is, free will] in the work of Adam, the First Man, was indeed according to "you shall choose the sweet," as mentioned above (16-4). And it turns out that the corporeal palate was all that was needed and [that] this was sufficient for him [Adam] to achieve all that was good for himself, that is, to know what the Creator had commanded him [to do] and what He had commanded him not to do.

הפרישה משקצים ורמשים, וכל אשר נפשו של אדם קצה בו, אנו
מקבלים שכר. והנך מוצא, שענין הבחירה, בעבודתו של אדה"ר אדם
הראשון, הי' היה ע"ד על דרך ובחרת במתוק כנ"ל (טז-4) כנזכר לעיל,
ונמצא שחיך הגופני לבד היה די ומספיק לו לכל תועלתו, לדעת
אשר צוה ה', ואשר לא צוהו.

# Chapter 17: Lies Have Short Wings

## The Craftiness of the Serpent

(17-1) Now we can understand the craftiness of the Serpent, in which, our sages have further informed us, Sama-kel (the Angel of Negativity) was embodied, and this is so because its words were extremely arrogant. And it opened by saying, "Even though the Creator did say, 'You shall not eat from all the trees of the garden...'" (Genesis 3:1) This means that [the Serpent] engaged in conversation [with Eve] because, as is known, the woman [herself] had not been ordered directly by the Creator, and this is why it [the Serpent] asked her about the "ways of discerning." In other words, how did she know that the Tree of Knowledge of Good and Evil was forbidden? Maybe all the fruit of the Garden was also forbidden to them? "And the woman said [to the Serpent], 'We may eat of the fruit of the trees of the garden, etc., and the Tree of Knowledge of Good and Evil you should not eat, neither shall you touch it, lest you die.'" (Genesis 3:2-3)

(17-2) There are two specific issues here: 1) Touching [the Tree of Knowledge], which was never forbidden [by the Creator]. Why then did she add this prohibition? 2) She had doubts in the words of the Creator, Heaven forbid; the Creator had [originally] said, "You shall surely die," but the woman said, "Lest you die." Could it be that she did not believe in the words of the Creator, Heaven forbid, even before the sin? Surely the woman answered according to the question of the Serpent. She was aware of what the Creator had prohibited, since all of the trees of the Garden were sweet and pleasant and [their fruit] fit to be eaten. But [this was] not so [with] the Tree [of Good and Evil] that was inside the Garden, which she was already close to touching, and she tasted with that [that is, just by being close] a taste that was as harsh as death.

(17-3) So she experienced on her own, through her own discerning, that there was a possibility of death even by touch, [and] therefore

# פרק יז: לשקר אין רגלים

## ערמת הנחש

(יז-1) ועתה, נבין ערמת הנחש, אשר חז"ל הוסיפו להודיענו, אשר הס"מ סטרא מסאבותא (צד הזוהמה) היה מתלבש בו, והיינו מפני שגבהו דבריו מאד. והנה פתח, באף כי אמר אלהי"ם לא תאכלו מכל עץ הגן (בראשית ג, א), פי' פירוש שנכנס עמה בדברים, להיות שהאשה לא נצטוה מפי הקב"ה הקדוש ברוך הוא, וע"כ ועל כן שאל אותה על דרכי הבירור, כלומר מאין תדע, שנאסר העצה"ד העץ הדעת. אולי נאסרו לכם גם כל פירות הגן. ותאמר האשה מפרי עץ הגן נאכל וכו', [ועץ הדעת טוב ורע] לא תאכלו ממנו ולא תגעו בו פן תמותון (בראשית ג, ב-ג).

(יז-2) ויש כאן ב' דיוקים גדולים, א' הא הנגיעה, לא נאסרה מעולם, ועל מה הוסיפה באיסור, ב', כי הטילה ספק בדברי השי"ת ח"ו חס ושלום, שהשי"ת שהשם יתברך אמר מות תמותון, והאשה אמרה פן תמותון, והיתכן שלא האמינה ח"ו חס ושלום בדבר ה', עוד מטרם החטא. אמנם האשה ענתה לו על פי שאלתו של הנחש, דעל כן יודעה, מה שאסר ה' כי כל עצי הגן מתוקים ונחמדים, וראוים לאכול, משא"כ מה שאין כן זה העץ אשר בתוך הגן, כבר היתה בו בקרוב לנגיעה, וטעמה בזה טעם קשה כמות.

(יז-3) והיא שהוכיחה מעצמה, שמצד הבירור שלה, יש חשש מיתה אפי' אפילו על הנגיעה ולכן הוסיפה להבין במצוות האיסור,

she understood more deeply the Precept of the prohibition on top of what she had heard from her husband because no one is wiser than an experienced one. And "lest you die" refers to the touching. Moreover, it seems that her answer [to the Serpent] was completely reasonable because who can interfere and deny a friend's sense of taste? Yet the Serpent denied it and said, "You will not die, for the Creator knows that on the day you eat of it, your eyes will be opened, etc." (Genesis 3:4-5)

## Opening the Eyes

(17-4) We have to be precise here. What has the subject of the Opening of the Eyes do here? Indeed, something new and higher than [her consciousness] did [the Serpent] inform her. [The Serpent] demonstrated to them that it was silly to think that the Creator had created something evil and harmful in His world. Surely, [the Serpent told her,] from the side of the Creator, this cannot be an evil and harmful matter. Rather, this bitterness that you taste in [the fruit], even when you get so close that you might touch it, is only from your side. This is because the purpose of eating [the fruit] is to make you realize how high your *komah* (stature) is. Therefore, you need extra holiness during the action so that your sole intention is to give pleasure to the Creator, thereby fulfilling the purpose for which you were created. And therefore, it seems to you that it is evil and harmful [but] only so that you [can] understand the extra holiness that is required of you.

(17-5) Indeed, "on the day you eat of it, etc." (Genesis 3:5) means that if your action is performed in holy [consciousness] and in purity and [is] clear as daylight, then "you will be like the Creator, knowing good and evil." This means that just as [the Tree of Knowledge] is surely for the Creator sweet in [its] absolute affinity [with Him], so also the good and bad would be for you, in absolute affinity, sweet and delightful. [Now] there is still room [at this point] to

על מה ששמעה מבעלה, כי אין חכם כבעל נסיון, ופן תמותון סובב
על הנגיעה. וכנראה, שהתשובה היה מספקת לגמרי, כי מי יתערב
ויכחיש בחוש הטעם של חבירו. אמנם הנחש הכחיש אותה, ואמר,
לא מות תמותון, כי יודע אלהי"ם כי ביום אכלכם ממנו ונפקחו
עיניכם וכו' (בראשית ג, ה).

## פקיחת עיניים

(יז-4) ויש לדייק, מה ענין פקיחת עינים לכאן, אמנם כן דבר חדש
ונשגב הימנה, הודיע אותה, שהוכיח להם, שטפשות היא לחשוב,
שברא ה' דבר רע ומזיק בעולמו, והא ודאי כלפי השי"ת *השם יתברך*
אין זה ענין רע ומזיק, אלא זה המרירות שתטעמו בו אפי' *אפילו*
בקירוב נגיעה, הוא רק מצדכם, להיות אכילה זו, הוא להעמיד
אתכם, על גובה מעלתכם, וע"כ *ועל כן* לקדושה יתירה אתם צריכים,
בעת המעשה שיהיה כל כונתכם להשפיע נ"ר *נחת רוח לו ית'* יתברך,
לקיים הכוונה שעליה נבראתם. ולפיכך הוא נדמה לכם כרע ומזיק,
כדי שתבינו הקדושה היתרה הנדרש מכם.

(יז-5) אמנם ביום אכלכם ממנו, פי' *פירוש*, אם תהיה המעשה
בקדושה וטהרה, ברורה כיום, אז והיתם כאלה"ם יודעי טוב ורע
(בראשית ג, ה), כלומר, כמו שכלפי השי"ת *השם יתברך* הוא ודאי מתוק
בהשואה גמורה, כן יהיה לכם הטוב והרע בהשואה גמורה, למתוק
ולעדן. ועדיין נשאר מקום להרהר באימון הנחש, מפני שהשי"ת

contemplate the reliability of the Serpent's words, since the Creator did not inform [Adam and Eve] of all this Himself. This is why the Serpent proceeded and said, "For the Creator knows that on the day you eat of it, your eyes will be opened." (ibid)

(17-6) [And the Serpent continued with:] "This means that from the Creator's side, it was superfluous to inform you of this. He knew that if you put your attention to this, that is, to eat from the aspect of holy consciousness, your eyes would be opened on their own to the understanding of the greatness of His exaltedness because you would feel in Him a miraculous sweetness and delicacy. For this reason, He did not need to inform you, and it is for this reason that He instilled in you the power of discerning, so that you would know on your own what benefits you."

## The Right Intention

(17-7) [The Scripture] says immediately afterward that "the woman saw that the tree was good for food and that it was a delight to the eyes, etc." (Genesis 3:6) This means that she did not rely on [the Serpent's] words but went and investigated on her own, using her own intelligence and understanding. She dedicated herself with great sanctity to give pleasure to the Creator in order to fulfill the purpose that was expected of her, and not at all for her own enjoyment. Then her eyes were opened, as the Serpent had said. And "the woman saw that the tree was good for food," (ibid.) which means that through seeing that it was "a delight to the eyes"—that is to say, even before she touched it—she felt a sweetness and a great desire; just by looking with her eyes, she saw that such pleasure had not been accorded to her so far with regard to all the other trees in the garden.

(17-8) She further learned that "the tree was to be desired to make one wise." (Genesis 3:6) In other words, there was in this tree a selfish pleasure and delight from afar, more than in any other tree in the

שהשם יתברך לא הודיעו זה בעצמו, ע"כ על כן הקדים הנחש, ואמר, כי יודע אלהי"ם כי ביום אכלכם ממנו, ונפקחו עיניכם (שם).

(יז-6) כלומר, מצד השי"ת השם יתברך דבר יתר הוא, להודיעכם זאת, להיותו יודע שאם תשימו לבבכם לזה, לאכל על צד הקדושה, ונפקחו עיניכם מעצמיכם, להבין גודל הרוממות שבו, כי תרגישו בו מתיקות ועידון עד להפליא, וא"כ ואם כן אינו צריך להודיעכם, דעל כן הטביע בכם כח המברר. לידע תועלתכם מעצמכם.

## כוונה נכונה

(יז-7) ומיד כתיב, ותרא האשה כי טוב העץ למאכל וכי תאוה הוא לעינים וכו' (בראשית ג, ו), פי' פירוש שלא סמכה עצמה על דבריו, אלא שהלכה ובררה מדעתה ותבונתה, והקדישה את עצמה בקדושה יתירה, לעשות נ"ר נחת רוח להשי"ת להשם יתברך, כדי להשלים הכונה הנרצה הימנה, ולא כלל להנאתה עצמה. שאז, נפקחו עיניה, כדברי הנחש, ותרא האשה כי טוב העץ למאכל (שם), והיינו ע"י על ידי זה שראתה, כי תאוה הוא לעינים, כלומר, דעוד מטרם שנגעה בו, הרגישה מתיקות ותאוה גדולה, בראות עיניה לבד שחמדה כזה עוד לא קרה לה, בכל עצי הגן.

(יז-8) ונתברר לה עוד, אשר נחמד העץ להשכיל (בראשית ג, ו), כלומר, דע"כ דעל כן שעל כן יש בעץ הזה תאוה וחמדה מרחוק, יתר מכל עצי הגן, היינו להשכיל עליו, אשר בשביל מעשה האכילה הזו,

garden. That is to say that she would have learnt from it, that it was for the sake of this action of eating that [Adam and she] had been created. And this was the entire purpose, as the Serpent revealed to her. So then, after this full investigation and discernment, "she took of its fruit and ate, and she also gave some to her husband with her, and he ate." (ibid) And the Scripture is careful to say "with her," indicating her pure intention, that is to say, only to share and not for her own sake. This is what the verse means when it says that she gave it "to her husband with her," that is, with her [together] in holiness.

*wow!
"snow job!"
What a*

נבראו, והוא כל המטרה, כמו שגילה לה הנחש. ואז, אחר הבירורין המוחלטים האלו, ותקח מפריו ותאכל, ותתן גם לאישה עמה ויאכל (שם), ודייק הכתוב במלת עמה, כלומר, על כונתה הטהורה, דהיינו רק להשפיע, ולא לצרכי עצמו וזה הוראת הכתוב, שנתנה לאישה עמה, כלומר, עמה בקדושה.

# Chapter 18: Immortality

## A Good Lie Beings With Truth

(18-1) Now we will get to the heart of the matter and the mistake that was associated with his leg. This Tree of Knowledge of Good and Evil was already mixed together with the aspect of the Vacant Space, that is to say, of the Form of magnitude of the [Desire to] Receive. It is [on this Form] that the *Tzimtzum* (Contraction) occurred, and the Supernal Light had already departed from there, as was discussed above (13-3). And it has already been explained (ibid) that Adam, the First Man, did not have in his structure Form of magnitude of the [Desire to] Receive that extended from the Vacant Space; but rather, it extended in its entirety from the System of Holiness, whose whole purpose is to bestow. This is according to what is said in the *Zohar* in the portion of *Kedoshim* (verse 62), regarding Adam, the First Man: "Adam had not one thing from this world," (see there), and therefore, the Tree of Knowledge was forbidden to him, just as [Adam's] root and the entire System of Holiness are separated from the *Sitra Achra* (Other Side) due to their Difference of Form, which is the matter of the separation, as was spoken of earlier (6-8). Therefore, he [Adam] was also commanded regarding [the Tree of Knowledge], and [he] was warned not to connect to it because if he did so, he would be separated from his holy root and die, just like the *Sitra Achra* and the *klippot (shells)*, which are dead because of their opposition to and separation from the [System of] Holiness and the source of life, as mentioned earlier.

(18-2) Indeed, Satan, who is Sama-kel or the Angel of Death, clothed himself as the Serpent and came down to seduce Eve with his lies, "You will not die." (Genesis 3:4) But because it is known that a lie that is not preceded by a word of truth does not come to exist, [the Serpent] therefore preceded the lie with a word of truth and revealed the purpose of Creation to her; that its entire purpose was to correct this Tree [of Knowledge], that is, to transform the big

# פרק יח: חיי נצח

### הרוצה לשקר יתחיל באמת

(חי-1) **ועתה** נבוא לעומק הענין, והטעות, שהיה קשור ברגלו, כי זה העצה"ד העץ הדעת טו"ר טוב ורע, היה מעורב מבחי' מבחינת חלל הפנוי, כלומר, מצורת הגדלות שבקבלה. שעליה היה הצמצום, ואור העליון כבר נפרד משם, כנ"ל (יג-3). וכבר נתבאר (שם), שאדם הראשון, לא היה לו כלל בבנינו, צורת גדלות הקבלה, הנמשך מחלל הפנוי, אלא כולו נמשך ממערכת הקדושה, שענינם להשפיע. כמו"ש כמו שכתוב בזוהר [פרשת] קדושים (סעיף סב'), דאדה"ר דאדם הראשון לא הוה לי' מהאי עלמא כלום לא היה לו מהעולם הזה כלום, ע"ש עיין שם. וע"כ ועל כן נאסר לו העצה"ד העץ הדעת, כמו ששורשו, וכל מערכת הקדושה, שהמה נפרדים מהס"א מהסטרא אחרא, (הצד האחר), משום שינוי הצורה שלהם, שהיא ענין הפירוד כנ"ל כנזכר לעיל (ו-8), וע"כ ועל כן גם הוא נצטוה עליו, והוזהר מלהתחבר בו, כי יופרד מחמתו משורשו, הקדוש, - וימות, כמו הס"א הסטרא אחרא והקלי' והקליפה שהמה מתים, לסבת הפכיותם ופירודם מהקדושה, וחי החיים, כנ"ל.

(חי-2) אמנם, השטן הוא הס"מ הסיטרא מסאבותא (צד הזוהמה) הוא המה"מ המלאך המות, שנתלבש בהנחש, וירד והסיתה לחוה, בדבר שקר שבפיו, לא מות תמותון (בראשית ג', ד'). ונודע, שכל דבר שקר שאין אומרים דבר אמת בתחילתו אינו מתקיים, וע"כ ועל כן הקדים אותה בדבר אמת, וגילה לה מטרת הבריאה, שכל ענינה לא באה,

Vessels of Receiving to the aspect of Sharing. This is the meaning of
the words of the sages who said that he [the Serpent] told her, "The
Creator ate from this tree and created the world," (*Midrash Rabbah*,
Genesis 19:4) meaning that He [the Creator] looked at this matter
from the aspect of "culmination of an action starts with a thought"
and this is why He created the world.

(18-3) As was made clear above (6-8), the first *Tzimtzum*
(Contraction) was only for the sake of mankind, who will
eventually make the Form of Receiving similar to that of Sharing;
see above (6-11) and this is true. Therefore, this was an opportunity
for [the Serpent], and the woman believed him. And while she
prepared herself to receive and enjoy only For the Sake of Sharing,
it happened that the Evil departed from the Tree of Knowledge of
Good and Evil, and it remained the Tree of Knowledge of Good.
[This occurred] because the whole idea of evil [in the Tree] was
there only from the aspect of Difference of Form, that is, of the
Receiving for the Self [Alone] that had been imprinted in it. But
by Receiving for the Sake of Sharing, [the woman] brought [the
Tree of Knowledge] to the ultimate purpose of its perfection, and
thus she performed the great *yichud* (unification), the kind that is
worthy of being at the culmination of an action.

## The Root of Addictions

(18-4) However, this [action of] Supernal Holiness was still before
its time because she [the woman] was not worthy of withstanding
it, except for the first bite but not for the second bite. (This is the
secret meaning of the passage in the *Zohar* that all [the Serpent's]

words are lies). Let me explain to you that there is no comparison
between someone who renounces a desire before he has tasted it
and become used to it and someone who renounces a desire after
having tasted it and becoming attached to it. Surely the first person
can [easily] renounce [his desire] once and for all, but this will not
be the case for the second person, who must work extremely hard to
renounce his desire little by little until this objective is completed.

אלא לתקן העץ הזה, כלומר, כדי להפך כלי קבלה הגדולים על צד ההשפעה, וז"ש וזה שאמרו חז"ל שאמר לה, אשר אלהי"ם אכל מעץ הזה וברא את העולם (מדרש רבה, בראשית, יט', ד'), כלומר, שהסתכל על ענין זה בבחי' בחינת סוף מעשה במחשבה תחילה וע"כ ועל כן ברא העולם.

(חי-3) וכמו שנתבאר לעיל (1-8), דכל ענין הצמצום א', לא היה אלא בשביל האדם, העתיד להשוות הצורה של קבלה, להשפעה, עי' עיין לעיל (1-11), והוא דבר אמת. וע"כ ועל כן היה השעה משחקת לו, והאשה האמינה אותו, בשעה שהשכינה את עצמה לקבל ולהנות רק בע"מ בעל מנת להשפיע, נמצא ממילא, שפרח הרע מן העצה"ד העץ הדעת טו"ר טוב ורע ונשאר עצה"ד עץ הדעת טוב. להיות שכל ענין הרע דשם, הוא רק מבחי' בחינת שינוי צורה, דקבלה לעצמו, שהיה מוטבע בו להטביע, אמנם בקבלה ע"מ על מנת להשפיע, הרי הביאתו על תכלית שלימותו, ונמצאת שעשתה יחוד הגדול, כמו שראוי להיות בסוף מעשה.

## שורש ההתמכרויות

(חי-4) אמנם זה הקדושה העליונה, היה עדיין שלא בעונתו, שלא היתה ראויה לעמוד בה, זולת באכילה א', אבל לא באכילה הב' (שז"ס שזה סוד [מה שכתב] הזוה"ק הזהר הקדוש דכלא מלילא בשיקרא שכל דבריו [של הנחש] הם שקר). ואסביר לך, כי אינו דומה, המנזר עצמו מהתאוה, בטרם שטעמה והורגל בה, להמנזר עצמו מהתאוה, אחר שטעמה ונקשר בה, כי הראשון ודאי יכול להזיר את עצמו, בפעם א' על תמיד, משא"כ מה שאין כן השני, צריך לעבודה יתירה, לפרוש מתאותו לאט לאט, עד שגומר הענין.

(18-5) Such was the case here: Because the woman had not yet tasted from the Tree of Knowledge and because she was [also] completely in the state of sharing, therefore it was easy for her to have the first bite for the sake of giving pleasure to the Creator in complete purity [lit. holiness]. But this is not the case after she tasted it because then she had already become attached to it with great desire and excessive craving for the Tree of Knowledge, to the point where she was no longer capable of renouncing that desire because it was no longer in her control. And this is what our sages [meant when they] said that "they have eaten it prematurely," that is, before it was ripe, that is, before they gained the power and might to control their own desires; understand this well.

(18-6) This is just like what our sages said in Tractate *Yevamot* (39b) on behalf of Abba Shaul, who said, "He who marries his brother's widow for the sake of her beauty or for the sake of sexual desire is like someone who commits incest." And [our sages] said, "The first mating is a decree but does it apply to the second time as well?" Study that well.

(18-7) And this is what is meant by the passage: "I have eaten, and I shall eat more," (*Midrash Beresheet Rabbah* 19:12) which means that even at the very same time that [Adam] very clearly heard that the Creator was angry with him, still he could not desist from it because a selfish desire had already taken hold of him. So it turns out that the first bite was from the aspect of the Holiness, but the second bite was in great defilement.

## Immortality, Drop by Drop

(18-8) This makes the severity of the punishment related to the Tree of Knowledge understandable: All humankind (lit. the children of Adam) gathering because of it [had] to die. Indeed, this death is a consequence of [lit. extended from] eating from it, as the Creator had warned [Adam], "On the day that you eat of it, you

(חי-5) כן הדבר הזה, להיות שהאשה עדיין לא טעמה מעצה"ד מעץ הדעת, והיתה כולה בבחי' בחינת השפעה, ע"כ על כן, בקל היה מעשיה לאכול אכילה ראשונה, ע"מ על מנת להשפיע נ"ר נחת רוח להשי"ת להשם יתברך בתכלית הקדושה, משא"כ מה שאין כן אחר שטעמה אותו, כבר נקשר בה תאוה גדולה וחמדה יתירה לעצה"ד לעץ הדעת, עד שלא היתה יכולה עוד לפרוש מתאוותה, כי כבר יצא הענין מרשותה. והיינו שאמרו חז"ל שאכלו פגה, פי' פירוש, טרם בישולו, דהיינו בטרם שקנו הכח והגבורה למשול על יצרם, והבן היטב.

(חי-6) ודומה למה שאמרו ז"ל במס' במסכת יבמות [דף לט' עמוד ב'] אליבא בשם דאבא שאול, שאמר, הנושא יבמתו לשם נוי ולשם אישות הוי כפוגע בערוה, ואמרו גזירה ביאה ראשונה אטו ביאה שניה, עש"ה עיין שם היטב.

(חי-7) וז"ש וזה שאמרו [חכמינו] ז"ל (בראשית רבא יט', יב'), אכלתי, ואוכל עוד, כלומר, שאפי' שאפילו בו בעת, שכבר שמע בפירוש, שחרה בו השי"ת השם יתברך, מ"מ מכל מקום לא יכול לפרוש הימנו, שכבר נקשר בו התאוה. ונמצא, שאכילה א', היה ע"ץ על צד הקדושה, ואכילה ב', היה בזוהמא גדולה.

## חיי נצח טיפין טיפין

(חי-8) ובזה מובן חומר ענשו של עצה"ד עץ הדעת, שנתקבצו עליו כל בני אדם למיתה, אמנם זה המיתה, נמשך מתוך אכילתו, כמו שהזהיר אותו השי"ת השם יתברך, ביום אכלך ממנו מות תמות (בראשית ב, יז). והענין להיות שנמשך לתוך איבריו, צורת גדלות הקבלה מחלל

shall surely die." (Genesis 2:17) And the reason is that the Form of Total Receiving that originated from the Vacant Space, which appeared from the *Tzimtzum* (Contraction) onwards, spread out through [Adam's] limbs. And [as a result,] the Supernal Light could not be as one with it [this form]. Therefore, this Eternal breath of life, which is described in the passage, "And the Creator breathed into his nostrils the breath of life, etc.," (Genesis 2:7) had to depart from there, and so his temporary livelihood became dependent on a piece of bread.

(18-9) And this life was not eternal life, as was previously intended for his [man's] needs, but is relatively similar to the "sweat' of life." That is to say that life would be divided for him into small drops, in such a way that each and every drop would be a part of his previous life. [These drops] are the sparks of the souls that would be divided among all [Adam's] descendants, to such a point that all his descendants—counting all the residents of [all] the settlements and all the generations all the way till the last generation—who fulfill the purpose of Creation are all one long chain. This means that the actions of the Creator did not change at all due to the sin of the Tree of Knowledge.

## Reincarnation

(18-10) But this Light of Life, which Adam, the First Man, contained in its entirety, became extended [after the sin] and was made longer into a chain that keeps on reincarnating according to the wheel of the changing of the forms, all the way to the End of the Correction, with no stopping at all, not even for one moment. This is because the actions of the Creator must be alive and continuously exist, since Holiness is always increased and never decreased. Understand that well.

הפנוי, אשר מצמצום ולהלן, כבר אור העליון א"א אי אפשר לו להיות עמה, בכפיפה אחת, וע"כ ועל כן זה הנשמת חיים הנצחית, המפורש בהכתוב, ויפח ה' באפו נשמת חיים (בראשית ז') מוכרח להסתלק משם, ונתלה לו חייתו הזמנית בפת לחם.

(חי-9) וחיים האלו, אינם חיים נצחיים כלמפרע, שהיה לצורכו עצמו, אלא דומה בערך, לזיעה של חיים, כלומר שנתחלק לו החיים לטפין טפין, באופן שכל טפה וטפה, הוא חלק מהחיים שלו הקודמים, שה"ע שהוא ענין ניצוצי נשמות שנתחלקו לכל תולדותיו עד שבכל תולדותיו, מכל בני הישוב ומכל הדורות, עד דור האחרון, המשלים מטרת הבריאה, המה, בערך שלשלת גדולה אחת, באופן שמעשי השי"ת השם יתברך לא נשתנו כלל וכלל, מחמת חטאו של עצה"ד עץ הדעת.

## גלגול נשמות

(חי-10) אלא זה האור החיים, שהיה בא"ר באדם הראשון בבת אחת, נמשך ונארך, לשלשלת גדולה המתגלגלת, על גלגל שינוי הצורות, עד גמר התיקון, בלי הפסק כלל כרגע, להיות מעשה ה' מוכרחין להיות חיים וקיימים, ומעלין בקודש ואין מורידין, והבן זה היטב.

(18-11) And just as it happened in the case of Adam, so, too, it has happened to all the people of the world together with him: Everyone has fallen from the eternal and collective aspect [of Holiness], according to the wheel of the changing of form, like what [had happened to] Adam. [This is] because Adam [meaning mankind] and the world have both an inner and an external value, where the external [value] always goes up and down according to the inner [value]; here, however, is not the place to talk about this at length. And this is what is meant by "by the sweat of your brow [lit. nose], you shall eat bread" (Genesis 3:19): that instead of the primary breath of life that the Creator blew into Adam's nostrils, now he has the "drop of sweat of life" in his nostrils.

WOW!

(חי-11) וכמקרה האדם, כן קרה לכל בני העולם עמו, כי כלם ירדו מבחי׳ מבחינה נצחית וכללית, על גלגל שינוי הצורה, כמו האדם , כי האדם ועולם, ערך פנימי וחיצון להם, אשר החיצונית תמיד עולה ויורד בהתאם להפנימי, ואכמ״ל ואין כאן מקומו להאריך. וז״ע וזה ענין בזיעת אפיך תאכל לחם (בראשית ג, יט), שבמקום נשמת החיים הקדום, שנפח ה׳ באפו, נמצא עתה, זיעה של חיים באפו.

# Chapter 19: The Negative System of the Klipot (Shells)

## Two Damages

(19-1) And this is what our sages have told us (Tractate *Bava Batra*, 17), "This is the Evil Inclination; this is Satan; this is the Angel of Death, which comes down and incites, then goes up and prosecutes, and then comes and takes away [the person's] soul." And this because two different kinds of overall damage were caused by the sin of the Tree of Knowledge. The first damage is that he [Satan] goes up and prosecutes. After [Adam] had been tempted to eat from the Tree of Knowledge and thus acquired into the structure of his body a Receiving Vessel of the Vacant Space, hatred and separation appeared between the Light of eternal life, which the Creator breathed into the nostrils of mankind, and the body of mankind.

(19-2) And this is according to what our sages said, "[Concerning] anyone who becomes proud, the Creator says: 'I and that person cannot live in the same place.'" (Tractate *Sotah* 5) This is because pride stems from the Receiving Vessel of the Vacant Space from which the Supernal Light had already departed and separated itself ever since the time of the *Tzimtzum* (Contraction) onwards, as the Holy *Zohar* says that the Creator detests the bodies that are structured for their own self. Therefore, the Light of life departed from [Adam]. And this is the first damage.

## 288 Sparks of Souls

(19-3) And the second damage is the falling of 288 sparks, which were already connected to the System of Holiness, as was discussed above (at the end of verse 13). But now, in order for the world not to be destroyed, they were handed over and descended to the System of the *Sitra Achra* (Other Side) and the *klippot (shells)*.

# פרק יט: המערכת השלילית של הקליפות

## שני קלקולים

(יט-1) **והיינו** שאמרו ז"ל [במסכת] ב"ב בבא בתרא [עמוד] י"ז], הוא היצה"ר היצר הרע **הוא השטן הוא מה"מ** המלאך המוות, **שיורד ומסית, ועולה ומקטרג, ובא ונוטל נשמתו. והוא, כי** ב' **קלקולים כוללים נעשו בסבת החטא של עצה"ד** עץ הדעת, **קלקול הא', ה"ע** הוא ענין **עולה ומקטרג, כי אחר שנתפתה ואכל מעצה"ד** מעץ הדעת, **וקנה בבנין גופו, כלי קבלה דחלל הפנוי, נעשה מחמת זה, שנאה והרחקה, בין אור החיים הנצחי דנפח ה' באפו של האדם ובין גוף האדם.**

(יט-2) **ודומה למה שאמרו** [חכמינו] **ז"ל כל המתגאה אומר הקב"ה** הקדוש ברוך הוא **אין אני והוא יכולין לדור במדור א'** (על פי מסכת סוטה ה'), **כי ענין הגאוה, נובעת מכלי קבלה דחלל הפנוי, שכבר אור העליון נתרחק ונפרד משם, מעת הצמצום ולהלן, ועד"ש** ועל דרך שכתוב **בזוהר הק'** הקדוש, **שהקב"ה** שהקדוש ברוך הוא **שונא את הגופות שבנינם אך לעצמם. וע"כ** ועל כן **פרח ממנו אור החיים והוא קלקול א'.**

## רפ"ח נצוצות

(יט-3) **וקלקול ב', הוא ירידת רפ"ח** (288) **ניצוצין, שכבר היו מחוברים במערכת הקדושה כנ"ל** (אות יג', בסוף), **שעתה, כדי שלא יחרב העולם, נמסרו וירדו, למערכת הס"א** הסיטרא אחרא (הצד האחר) **והקלי'** והקליפה.

(19-4) [The reason for this is] because the System of Holiness could not sustain and nourish Adam and the rest of mankind, due to the hatred that had arisen between the Holiness and the Vessels of the Vacant Space, in accordance with the law of being opposite to each other, as was stated above: "I and that [proud] person cannot be in the same place." Therefore, the 288 sparks were handed over to the System of the *Sitra Achra*, so that it [the Other Side] could nourish and sustain Adam and the world throughout the entire period of the reincarnation of the souls in bodies—600,000 [sparks of souls] in a generation, for 1000 generations—until the Correction is completed.

(19-5) Here you will understand why the *klippot (shells)* are referred to by that name. It is because their significance [lit. value] is similar to that of a shell of a fruit, since it is the hard shell that surrounds and covers the fruit to preserve it from any kind of filth and damage until the moment comes for the fruit to be eaten. For without [the shell], the fruit would be ruined and would not reach its purpose. So you find that the 288 sparks were handed over to the *klippot (shells)* in order to nourish and prepare the reality, until [the sparks] are united and achieve their desired goal, as mentioned above (13-9; 19-3).

## Stamp and Seal

(19-6) The second damage mentioned earlier is that [the *Sitra Achra* (Other Side)] comes and takes away [the person's] soul. What I mean is that even this small part of the soul that remains in a person as an aspect of [a drop of] sweat from previous lifetimes is stolen by the *Sitra Achra*. This is done by means of the same abundance that it [the *Sitra Achra*] bestows upon him from the 288 sparks, which have fallen to its lot. To understand this, you must picture the nature of the *Sitra Achra* as it is, so that you may learn all its ways. I have already shown in *Enlightening and Explaining Face*, branch 6, that all the parts of reality in the Lower World are branches that extend from their root in the Upper World, like a stamp from a seal: That the Upper World [extends] from the one higher [above it], and that one from the next higher yet, etc.

(יט-4) כי מאחר שאין מערכת הקדושה יכולה, לפרנס ולכלכל את האדם ובני העולם, מסבת השנאה, שנתהוה בין הקדושה והכלים דחלל הפנוי, כחוק ההפכים זה לזה, כנ"ל, שאין אני והוא יכולים לדור במדור א'. ע"כ על כן נמסרה הרפ"ח (288) ניצוצין למערכות הס"א הסיטרא אחרא (הצד האחר), כדי שהמה יכללו ויקיימו את האדם והעולם, בכל משך זמן גלגולי הנשמות בהגופים בס' (60) ריבוא לדור, ובאלף דור, עד גמר התיקון.

(יט-5) ובזה תבין, למה המה מכונים בשם קליפות, להיות ערכם, כערך הקליפה שעל הפרי, כי קליפה הקשה חופפת ומכסית על הפרי, לשמרה מכל טינוף והיזק, עד שתבוא הפרי, לידי האוכלה, שבלעדה, היה הפרי נשחתה, ולא היתה באה למטרתה. כן אתה מוצא, אשר הרפ"ח (288) ניצוצין נמסרו לידי הקליפות, כדי לכלכל ולהכשיר את המציאות, עד שיתחברו וישיגו למטרתם הנרצה, כנ"ל (יג-9; יט-3).

## חותם ונחתם

(יט-6) והנה קלקול הב' הנזכר, ה"ע הוא ענין ובא ונוטל נשמתו, רצוני לומר, גם זה החלק הקטן של נשמה, הנשאר לו להאדם, בבחי' בבחינת זיעה, של חיים הקודמים, הרי הס"א הסיטרא אחרא (הצד האחר) עושקתה, על ידי אותה ההשפעה בעצמה, שהיא משפעת לו מהרפ"ח (288) הניצוצין, שנפלו לגורלה. ולהבינך את זה, צריך לצייר היטב תמונת הס"א הסיטרא אחרא (הצד האחר) כמות שהיא, בכדי שתוכל להשכיל כל דרכיה, וכבר הראיתי לדעת בפמ"ס בפנים מסבירות בענף ו' דכל חלקי המציאות מעולם התחתון, המה ענפים נמשכים משרשם, כמו חותם מחותם, מעולם העליון, והעליון מגבוה הימנו, והגבוה, מגבוה על גבוה וכו'.

*reread this*

**(19-7)** You should know, too, that any difference between the Branches and the Roots stems only from the elements of the matter in them. That is to say, the matter in this World is composed of physical elements, while the matter in the World of *Yetzirah* (Formation) is composed of spiritual elements; in other words, from the aspect of the spirituality of *Yetzirah*. And it continues so, from one World to the next, each one from its own aspect [unique characteristic]. Indeed, the cases and processes in them have an equal value, from each branch to its root, just like two drops of water that are equal to each other, and just as a seal is similar in every respect to the stamp that created it. And once you know this, we can look for that branch that the upper *Sitra Achra* (Other Side) has in this World, and through that, we can also know the upper root of the *Sitra Achra*.

*Okay!*

## The Light of Pleasure is the Producer of Life

**(19-8)** In the *Zohar* portion of *Tazria* (verse 143), we find that afflictions in the body of mankind are branches of the upper *Sitra Achra* (Other Side); study that well. And so we can extrapolate the *komah* (stature) of the living being, where we find that what has sprouted inside his body by attaining pleasure is what augments and enhances his life. Therefore, Providence has instilled in small [children] the ability to find fulfillment and pleasure from whatever they set their eyes upon, even from the small and trifling things that have no value, because the *komah* of the small [child] demands a huge amount [of sustenance] of life for it to have fulfillment to enable his growth. And for this reason, their pleasure is easily available.

**(19-9)** And you find that the light of pleasure is the producer of life. However, this rule applies only to pleasure that is bestowed upon the entirety of the *komah* (stature). But when it comes to fragmented pleasure—that is, pleasure that is accumulated and felt only in one separate part of the *komah* of the living being—then we find that the opposite applies.

(יט-7) ותדע, שכל הבחן שיש מהענפים על השורשים, הוא רק ביסודות החומר שבהם לבד, כלומר שחומריים שבעוה"ז שבעולם הזה, המה יסודות גשמיים, והחומריים שבעולם היצירה המה יסודות רוחניים, דהיינו מבחי' מבחינת רוחניית היצירה, וכן כל עולם ועולם מבחינתו, אמנם המקרים וההתהלוכות שבהם, יש להם ערך שוה, מכל ענף לשורשו, כמו ב' טפות מים, השוות זו לזו, וכמו הנחתם ששוה צורתו בכל וכל להחותם, שממנו נחתם. ואחר שתדע זה, נבקש את זה הענף, שישנו להס"א הסיטרא אחרא (הצד האחר) העליונה בעוה"ז בעולם הזה, ואז נדע על ידו, גם את שורשו הס"א הסיטרא אחרא (הצד האחר) העליונה.

## אור התענוג הוא אבי החיים

(יט-8) ומצאנו בזוהר הק' הקדוש **פרשת תזריע** (הסולם, סעיף קמג'), דהנגעים שבגופי בני אדם, המה ענפים של הס"א הסיטרא אחרא (הצד האחר) העליונה עש"ה עיין שם היטב. ולפיכך, נקח להשכיל את קומת הבעל חי, ואנו מוצאים בו, אשר זה הנביע המתהוה בגופו, ע"י על ידי השגת התענוג, הוא המרבה ומפריא לו החיים, וע"כ ועל כן ההשגחה הטביעה בהקטנים, שבכל מקום שיתנו עיניהם, ימצאו קורת רוח ותענוג, ואפי' ואפילו מדברים קטנטנים של מה בכך. להיות קומת הקטן, מחוייב לרביה של חיים ביותר, כדי שיהיה סיפוק בו לצמיחה וגידול, וע"כ ועל כן תענוגם מצוי.

(יט-9) והנך מוצא אשר אור התענוג הוא אבי החיים. אמנם חוק זה, אינו נוהג זולת בתענוג, שהוא מושפע לכללות הקומה, אבל בתענוג דפרודא, כלומר, בהשתענוג מתקבץ ומקובל, רק לחלק נבדל של קומת הבעל חי, אז אנו מוצאים בו דין הפוך.

## Level of Pleasure – Level of Pain

(19-10) This means that if [a person] has an affliction in his flesh, for example, something that needs to be rubbed and scratched, then this action of scratching does bring some reward with it because with it, he feels great pleasure that he pursues with great passion. Yet along with this pleasure, a drop of the potion of death follows because if he does not control his desire and [continues to] pay out this haunting demand, he will find that the payments actually increase his debt even more.

(19-11) This means that [in equal measure] to the level of pleasure that [the person] obtains from scratching, the affliction increases and the pleasure turns into pain. Then when it starts healing, a new demand for rubbing is born with it to a degree that is even greater than before. And if he still does not control his desire and again responds to the demand, the affliction [continues to] increase until in the end, it brings him a drop of bitterness, which poisons all the blood in that living being.

## Fragmented Source of Pleasure

(19-12) And so he ends up dying by receiving pleasure because [this pleasure] is a fragmented source of pleasure, which comes only to an isolated part of the *komah* (stature). This is why death operates in that [one part of the] *komah*, as opposed to the pleasure that is bestowed on the *komah* as a whole, as was said above. So [now] we can understand the upper Form of the *Sitra Achra* (Other Side) from head to toe [lit. ankle]. Its "head" is the Desire to Receive for the Self Alone and to not share anything outside of itself, which is like the demand of the afflicted flesh in comparison to the entire *komah* (stature) of the living being. And the "body" of the *Sitra Achra* is the sort of demand that can never be paid off because the more a person goes on paying, the more he increases the debt and the affliction, just as in the example of receiving pleasure through scratching, as we explained above (19-1).

## כגודל התענוג - גודל הכאב

(יט-10) דהיינו אם יש לו מקום לקוי בבשרו, התובע אותו לגרד ולחכך, והנה פעולת החיכוך, מביאה לו ג"כ גם כן שכרו בצדה, שמרגיש עמה תענוג מרובה ברדיפה כבירה, אמנם בתענוג זה, טפת סם המות כרוך בעקבו, שבאם לא ימשול על יצרו, וישלם את התביעה הרדופה, נמצאים התשלומים מגדילים עוד את חובו.

(יט-11) כלומר, לפי מדתו של השגת התענוג מהחיכוך, כן יתרבה עליו הלקותא, ויתהפך התענוג למכאוב, ובהתחילה שוב להתרפאות, נולד עמה יחד, תביעה חדשה לחיכוך, ובמדה יותר גדולה מקודם, ואם עדיין אינו מושל ביצרו, ושוב משלם די התביעה, נמצא גם הלקותא הולך ומתרבה עליו, עד שמביאה לו טפה של מרה בסופו, שמרעלת כל הדם, שבאותו החי.

## תענוג דפרודא

(יט-12) ונמצא, שמת ע"י על ידי קבלת התענוג, מפני שהיא תענוג דפרודא, המקובל רק לחלק נבדל של הקומה, וע"כ ועל כן פועלת המות בהקומה, בהפכי מהתענוג המושפע לכלל הקומה, כאמור. והנה הגיע לפנינו, צורת הס"א הסיטרא אחרא (הצד האחר) העליונה מראשה עד עקבה, אשר ראשה, הוא הרצון לקבל אך לעצמה, ולא להשפיע מחוץ לה, כתכונת התביעה שבבשר המנוגע, בערך כללו של קומת החי; וגופה של הס"א הסיטרא אחרא (הצד האחר), היא צורתה של מין תביעה, שאינה עומדת להפרע, שהפרעון שהוא הולך ופורע, עוד מגדיל החוב והלקותא, ביותר, כדוגמת קבלת תענוג ע"י על ידי החיכוך, כנ"ל (יט-1) .

(19-13) And the toe [lit. ankle] of the *Sitra Achra* (Other Side) is the drop of the potion of death, which robs [the person] and severs him from even the last spark of life that is left to him, just like the drop of the potion of death mentioned above that poisons all the blood in the *komah* (stature) of the living being. And that is what our sages said, "And then [the Other Side] finally comes and collects his soul," as said above. And this is what [the sages] meant when they said that the Angel of Death comes by with a drawn sword and there is a bitter drop at the edge of that sword, and the person opens his mouth and [the Angel of Death] throws that drop into it, and [the person] dies. (Tractate *Avoda Zara* 20b)

(19-14) The sword of the Angel of Death is the influence of the *Sitra Achra*, which is called the "sword" because of the separation that increases with the degree of Receiving, and this separation destroys [in Hebrew, "sword" comes from the word "destroy"] him, as mentioned above (19-1). For the person is forced to open his mouth because he has no choice but to receive the abundance of sustenance for his existence from it, until the drop of bitterness at the end of the sword gets to him, which completes the separation from the last spark of his life-breath, as mentioned above (19-11).

*Wow!*

(יט-13) ועקבה של הס"א הסיטרא אחרא (הצד האחר), היא הטפה של סם המוות, שעושקתו ומפרידו, גם מניצוץ חיים האחרון שנשאר לו, כדוגמת טפה של סם המוות הנ"ל המרעלת את כל הדם שבקומת הבעל חי. והיינו שאמרו ז"ל ולבסוף בא ונוטל את נשמתו, כנ"ל. והיינו שאמרו (במסכת עבודה זרה, דף כ', עמוד ב'): שהמה"מ שמלאך המוות מזדמן בחרב שלופה וטפה של מרה בקצה החרב, והאדם פותח פיו וזורק בו הטפה, ומת.

(יט-14) אשר חרבו של מה"מ מלאך המוות, הוא השפעת הס"א הסיטרא אחרא (הצד האחר), שנק' שנקרא חרב, לסבת הפירוד המתגדל במדת הקבלה, שהפירוד מחריבו, כנ"ל (יט-1), והאדם פותח בהכרח את פיו, להיות שמוכרח לקבל שפע הקיום והעמדתו, מתחת ידיה. עד שמגיע אליו טפה של מרה, שבסוף החרב, שהוא גמר הפירוד לניצוץ האחרון של נשמת חייו, כנ"ל (יט-11).

## *Chapter 20: Two Opposites*

### From a Perfect Performer a Perfect Action is Drawn

(20-1) Because of these two kinds of damage, the structure of the body of the human being was also damaged, since it was adapted from the aspect of [the World of] *Yetzirah* (Formation) with utmost precision to receive the abundance for [the person's] existence from the System of Holiness. All the elements of every action that are performed with consent and are everlasting will be protected from any kind of [either] lack or redundancy. But an action that is performed with no consent and is not everlasting is this way because its parts are missing the right balance, and somewhere within it, there is something [either] missing or redundant.

(20-2) As it is said in *Shir Ha'Yichud* (*Song of the Unification*): "Of all your works, You have forgotten not one thing; You did not miss out or exaggerate in anything." This refers to the mandatory rule that from a perfect Performer, a perfect action is drawn. When mankind, however, crosses over from the System of Holiness to the System of the *Sitra Achra* (Other Side) and because of the attachment that was added to his [spiritual] structure through the [sin of the] Tree of Knowledge, as mentioned above (19.4), there are many parts in his body that are in redundancy and are not necessary. They do not receive anything from the abundance of existence that is bestowed upon them from the authority of the *Sitra Achra*, as we find in [the case of] the bone called "*luz*" (top of the spinal column); see in the *Zohar* in the *Midrash HaNe'elam*, *Toledot* (verses 50-51) and also the appendix (Tractate *Chulin* 50) and so forth. [This redundancy is also found] in specific parts of each and every organ, but this is not the place to expound [upon this matter].

# פרק כ: שני הפכים

## מפועל שלם יוצאת פעולה שלימה

(כ-1) ובסבת ב' הקלקולים הנ"ל נתקלקל ג"כ גם כן בנין גופו של אדם להיותו מותאם מצד היצירה, בתכלית הדיוק, לקבלת שפע של קיומו, ממערכת הקדושה. כי כל פעולה מאושרה, ושל קיימא, יהיו חלקיה משמורים, מהעדפה או מגרעת עד לכל שהוא, והפעולה שאינו מאושרה, ושאינה של קיימא, הוא בשביל, שחלקיה חסרי המזג, ומצוי בהם בכל שהוא מגרעת או העדפה.

(כ-2) וע"ד ועל דרך שאומר בשיר היחוד מכל מלאכתך דבר אחד לא שכחת, לא העדפת ולא החסרת. והוא חוק מחוייב, שמהפועל השלם נמשך פעולה שלימה. אמנם בעבור האדם, ממערכת הקדושה למערכת הס"א הסיטרא אחרא (הצד האחר), בסבת הספחת הנוסף בבנינו, ע"י על ידי העצה"ד העץ הדעת, כנ"ל (יט-4), כבר נמצאים חלקים מרובים בבנין גופו בעודפות, בלי צורך, להיותם אינם מקבלים כלום, משפע של קיום המושפע מרשות הס"א הסיטרא אחרא (הצד האחר). כמו שאנו מוצאים בעצם לוז עיין בזוהר במד' במדרש הנעלם [פרשת] תולדות (הסולם סעיפים נ'-נא') וכן סניא דיבי תוספתן (מסכת חולין, דף נ) וכו', וכן בחלק ידוע מכל אבר ואבר, ואכמ"ל (ואין כאן מקום להאריך).

## Overdose

(20-3) Therefore, a person must feed his body with more nourishment than is necessary because this above mentioned redundancy is connected to every demand that emerges from the body and [that] the body therefore receives on [this redundancy's] behalf. But the excess itself cannot receive its share, and therefore these [extraneous] parts remain in the body as extra material and waste, which the body then has to excrete. So the organs of eating and digesting are laboring for no avail on behalf of [these extraneous parts], and so [these digestive organs] gradually waste away until they die off. The reason for this is because their fate has already been decreed, as has that of every unbalanced action that is doomed eventually to fall apart. Thus you find that even from the perspective of the construction of the body, its death has been preordained by cause and effect from the Tree of Knowledge.

(20-4) By now, we have had the merit to learn and know about the two kinds of supervision [of reality] that are completely contradictory to each other, which we discussed in verse 11 (11-5); see there. The supervision of the existence and sustenance of the people of the reality [of this world] has already passed from the System of Holiness to the System of the *Sitra Achra* (Other Side). This is because of the attachment of the magnitude of the [Desire to] Receive for the Self Alone, which was connected to mankind as a consequence of the [sin of] eating from the Tree of Knowledge. This [sin] caused separation and hatred and polarity between the System of Holiness and the structure of the bodies of the people of the reality of This World. This is because the [System of] Holiness could no longer sustain and nourish them from a high table.

(20-5) Therefore, in order for the reality [of this world] not to be destroyed and in order to prepare a course for [mankind's] Correction, [the System of Holiness] handed over the entire abundance for the existence of this reality to the System of the *Sitra Achra* (Other Side). This is what the 288 sparks [of souls] is all about. Thus, [the System of the *Sitra Achra*] has become the provider for all the people of the world during the ongoing period of their *Tikkun* (Correction).

**מנת יתר**

(3-כ) ולפיכך מחויב האדם, לקבל כלכלה לתוך גופו, יתר מהצורך, להיות העודפות הנ"ל, מתחברים בכל תביעה, העולה מהגוף, וע"כ <sub>ועל כן</sub> מקבל הגוף בשבילם, אמנם העודפות בעצמם אינם יכולים לקבל חלקיהם, וע"כ <sub>ועל כן</sub> נשאר חלקיהם בגוף, בבחי' <sub>בבחינת</sub> מותרות ופסולת, שהגוף מחויב אח"כ <sub>אחר כך</sub> להפליט לחוץ. ונמצאים כלי המאכל והעיכול, מתייגעים לריק ולבטלה בשבילם, וע"כ <sub>ועל כן</sub> הולכים ונפסדים, עד לכליון, כי משפטם חרוץ ככל פעולה מחסרי המזג, שסופה להתפרק. והנך מוצא גם מצד בנין הגוף, שנתלה מיתתו, בקודם ונמשך מעצה"ד <sub>מעץ הדעת</sub>.

(4-כ) ועתה זכינו להשכיל ולדעת, בדבר ב' ההנהגות הסותרות זו את זו עד לקצה, שעמדנו עליהם, לעיל באות י"א ע"ש <sub>עיין שם</sub> (יא-5). כי הנהגת קיום וכלכלה של בני המציאות, כבר עברה ממערכת הקדושה למערכת הס"א <sub>הסיטרא אחרא (הצד האחר)</sub>, והוא, מסבת הספחת, של גדלות הרצון לקבל לעצמו, הנקשר בבני המציאות, מסבת אכילת העצה"ד <sub>העץ הדעת</sub>, שגרם פירוד והפכיות ושנאה, בין מערכת הקדושה, לבנין הגופות של בני מציאות העוה"ז <sub>העולם הזה</sub>. בשכבר הקדושה, אינה יכולה לקיימם ולזונם, משלחן גבוה.

(5-כ) וע"כ <sub>ועל כן</sub> כדי שלא יחרב המציאות, וכדי להזמין להם מהלך תיקונם, מסרתה לכללות השפע של קיום המציאות, שה"ע <sub>שהוא ענין</sub> רפ"ח (288) הניצוצין שלה, למערכת הס"א <sub>הסיטרא אחרא (הצד האחר)</sub>, שהמה יהיו המפרנסים לכל בני העולם בזמן המשך התיקונים.

## The Reason for the Confused Reality

(20-6) For this reason, the ways of existence are found to be very confused because from the wicked, evil emerges. And behold, if the abundance to the people of the world is reduced, it will surely bring chaos and suffering, and if the abundance is increased, then the recipients will feel that the power of separation is increased. This is according to what our sages said: "If [people] have a portion of one hundred, they want two hundred, and if they have two hundred, they want four hundred." (*Midrash Rabba, Kohelet*, A:3)

(20-7) This is similar to the fragmented source of pleasure, which is attained for the separated and afflicted flesh, as mentioned above (19:9-12), because the greater the pleasure, the more there is of separation and affliction. And it turns out that self-love [that is, the Desire to Receive for the Self Alone] increases greatly in the recipients, and [therefore] one person swallows the other alive. And the life of the body decreases as well, because through the increase of the amount of receiving, one quickly comes to the bitter drop [of death] at its end. Thus, wherever one turns, he finds damnation, as discussed above (20-3).

## Similarity of Form and Difference in Form

(20-8) Through this, you will understand what was said in the *Tosafot* (additional commentaries) to Tractate *Ketubot* page 104: That instead of praying for the Torah to enter their body, [people] should pray that no delicacies enter their body; see there. This is because the Form of Receiving for the Self Alone, which is the opposite of the [System of] Holiness, proliferates and grows at the [same] rate as the pleasure that [the person] attains for his body, as mentioned above (20-3). So how is it possible for us to attain the Light of the Torah into our body when we are separated by complete Difference of Form from the Holiness? And there is great hatred between the two, in the same way that all opposites hate each other and cannot exist under one roof.

## סיבת הבלבול והמבוכה

(כ-6) וע"כ וע'על כן סדרי הקיום נמצאים מבולבלים מאד, כי מרשעים יצא רשע, וממ"נ וממה נפשך, אם ממעיטים השפע לבני העולם, מביאים ודאי חורבן ויסורים, ואם מרבים בשפע נמצאים מביאים כח הפירוד ביותר להמקבלים, ע"ד על דרך שאמרו [חכמינו] ז"ל, יש לו מנה רוצה מאתים, ויש לו מאתים רוצה ארבע מאות (מדרש רבה, קהלת א עג').


(כ-7) כדמיון התענוג דפרודא, המושג לבשר הנפרד והלקוי הנ"ל (יט 9-12), שכמות התענוג, מרבה הפירוד והלקותא, ונמצא האהבה עצמיית, מתגבר ביותר בהמקבלים, ואיש את חבירו חיים בלעו, וגם חיי הגוף מתקצרים, כי ע"י על ידי ריבוי כמות הקבלה, מגיע במוקדם לטפה של מרה שבאחריתה, ובכל מקום שהם פונים, אך מרשיעים, כנ"ל (כ-3).


## שווי צורה והפכיות צורה

(כ-8) ובזה תבין, מ"ש מה שכתוב בתוספות [מסכת] כתובות דף ק"ד, דעד שאדם מתפלל שיכנס תורה לתוך גופו, יתפלל שלא יכנסו מעדנים לתוך גופו, ע"ש עיין שם. והיינו, משום דצורת הקבלה העצמיית, שהוא ההפכי מהקדושה מתרבה ומתגדל, בשיעור התענוג המושג לגופו, כנ"ל (כ-3). וא"כ ואם כן איך אפשר לו להשיג אור תורה לתוך גופו, בהיותו נפרד בהפכיות הצורה עד לקצה מהקדושה, ושנאה גדולה מצוי ביניהם, כערך כל ההפכיים ששונאים זה לזה, ואינם יכולים להמצא בכפיפה אחת.

(20-9) It is simple [to understand] that we should first pray for delicacies and pleasures not to enter our body. Thus, the more we are manifesting the Torah and the Precepts, the more we merit, step-by-step, transforming the Form of Receiving [for the Self Alone] to that [of Receiving] for the Sake of Sharing. And thereby, our [spiritual] Form is made similar to that of the System of Holiness, and the affinity returns together with the love between us, as it was before the sin of the Tree of Knowledge. And then we merit the Light of the Torah because we approach the presence of the Creator.

(כ-9) ופשוט הוא, שמחוייב מקודם להתפלל, שלא יכנסו המעדנים והתענוגים לתוך גופו, ולפי רוב המעשה בתורה ומצות, נמצא לאט לאט, זוכה להפך צורת הקבלה לע"מ לעל מנת להשפיע, ונמצא משוה צורתו למערכת הקדושה, וחזר להיות ההשתוות והאהבה ביניהם, כמו שהיה קודם חטאו של עצה"ד עץ הדעת, וזוכה לאור תורה, להיותו נכנס למחיצתו של הקב"ה הקדוש ברוך הוא.

# Chapter 21: Temporarity for the Sake of Eternity

## Angels Regret

(21-1) Now we can understand why the answers of the supernal angels regarding the creation of Adam [and mankind], which we discussed above in verse 11, were not given; see there. This is because even the Angels of Mercy and Righteousness could not agree about mankind of the present period [that is, after the sin of Adam] because [mankind] had completely passed from under [the angels'] influence and was now sustained by the *Sitra Achra* (Other Side), as discussed above (12-6).

(21-2) And that is why the *Midrash* concludes (11-3) by saying that [the Creator] took hold of [the Angel of] Truth and threw it to the earth (Daniel 8:12). Immediately all said, "May Truth spring forth from the earth," (Psalms 85:12) which is to say that even the Angels of Mercy and Righteousness regretted their consent [to the creation of the Man] because they never agreed for this to happen, namely, for Truth to be degraded.

(21-3) This situation occurred while [Adam and Eve were] eating of the Tree of Knowledge, as [the Angel of] Truth did not take part in the administration of the reality. It happened because the power of discerning, which was instilled in the human being from the aspect of [the World of] *Yetzirah* (Formation) and which functions by sensing bitter and sweet, as explained above in verse 16 (see there) became weak and failed. The reason for this [failure] is that the abundance, which [consists of] the 288 different aspects destined for existence, has already been refined and has become clear as the sun at noon and was connected to the System of Holiness. The palate that eats will savor the taste (Job 12:11), [both] to come close to everything that is beloved and sweet and to be completed by it, and to reject all that is bitter and bad for him, so that a person would not fail by it; study that well.

## פרק כא: זמניות לשם נצחיות

### מלאכים מתחרטים

(כא-1) **ועתה** מובן היטב, למה לא מובא תשובתם של המלאכי מעלה, בדבר בריאת האדם, שעמדנו בהמדרש כנ"ל, באות י"א ע"ש עיין שם. להיות, שעל אדם של עתה, לא הסכימו אפי' אפילו מלאכי חסד וצדקה, כי יצא כולו מתחת השפעתם, ונעשה סמוך על שלחן של הס"א הסיטרא אחרא (הצד האחר) כנ"ל (יב-6).

(כא-2) והיינו שמסיים המדרש (יא-3) , שנטל האמת והשליכו לארץ (דניאל ח', יב'), מיד אמרו כולם תעלה האמת מן הארץ (תהלים פה, יב'). כלומר, שאפי' אפילו מלאכי חסד וצדקה, התחרטו על הסכמתם, כי אדעתא דהכי לא הסכימו מעולם, שיתבזה האמת וכו'.

(כא-3) שמקרה הזה, קרה בעת אכילת העצה"ד העץ הדעת, שנעדר האמת מהנהגת קיום המציאות, כי נכשל ונחלש כח הבירור, המוטבע באדם מצד היצירה, שאופני פעולתו, היה ע"י על ידי הרגש מר ומתוק, כמו"ש כמו שכתוב לעיל באות ט"ז, עש"ה עיין שם הכתוב. כי השפע של קיום, שהם רפ"ח (288) בחי' בחינות שונות, כבר היו ברורים, כשמש בצהרים, ומחוברים במערכת הקדושה, "וחיך אוכל יטעם" (איוב יב יא), לקרב ולהשתלם, בכל הנאהב והמתוק, ולדחות כל המר, והרע לו, באופן שלא יכשל אדם בהם, כנ"ל עש"ה עיין שם היטב.

## Sweet Beginning With a Bitter End

(21-4) Indeed, after the first taste of the Tree of Knowledge, the Form of Total Receiving for the Self Alone was attached to [Adam and Eve], and their body and the Holiness became two opposites, as discussed above (19-1). Then the abundance [intended] for existence, which is the 288 aspects mentioned above (13), was passed on to the *Sitra Achra* (Other Side). And so the 288 sparks, which had already been discerned from before, were again mixed up by the *Sitra Achra*.

(21-5) As a result, a new form was born in [our] reality, which was the Form [of Receiving] that starts sweet and ends bitter. For it is in this manner that the Form [of Receiving] of the 288 sparks was changed by the *Sitra Achra*, and so the Light of Delight became the conduit through which separation and the drop of bitterness were brought about, as mentioned above (19-3). And this is the 'Form of Falsehood,' the source [lit. father] of all chaos and all confusion.

(21-6) This is why it is said that (verse 11): "He took the Truth and threw it to earth," and therefore, because of the Serpent, a new power of discerning was instilled in Man. This [power of discerning] is the active force of the mind that acts by discerning the true from the false, and is obliged to serve him throughout the process of the Correction. Without [being able to discern truth from falsehood], any benefit is obstructed, as mentioned above in verse 16; study that well.

## "I Have Eaten, and I Shall Eat More"

(21-7) Come and learn the amount of confusion that was created due to the fall of the 288 sparks into the hands of the *Sitra Achra* (Other Side). Before tasting from the Tree of Knowledge, the woman could not even touch that which was forbidden, as discussed above in verse 17, because when she came even close to touching the Tree of Knowledge, she immediately tasted in it a bitterness that tasted like death. Because of this, she understood and added

## התחלה מתוקה וסוף מר

(כא-4) אמנם אחר הטעימה הראשונה של עצה"ד עץ הדעת, שבחמתה נתדבק בהם, צורת גדלות הקבלה העצמיית, ונעשה גופם עם הקדושה, ב' הפכים, כנ"ל (יט-1). אז הגיע השפע של קיום, שהיא רפ"ח (288) הבחי' בחינות הנ"ל (סעיף יג), לידי הס"א הסיטרא אחרא (הצד האחר). ונמצא שרפ"ח (288) הניצוצין, שהיו כבר ברורים, חזרו ונתבלבלו בידי הס"א הסיטרא אחרא (הצד האחר).

(כא-5) ונולד צורה חדשה במציאות, שה"ע שהוא עניין הצורה, שתחילתה מתוק וסופה מר. כי כן נשתנה, צורת הרפ"ח (288) בידי הס"א הסיטרא אחרא (הצד האחר), שאור התענוג, שעל ידיהם מביא פירוד, וטפה של מרה של מרה כנ"ל (יט-13). שזה הוא צורת השקר, אבי אבות החורבנות וכל בלבול.

(כא-6) וז"ש וזה שאמר (סעיף יא) שנטל האמת והשליכו לארץ, וע"כ ועל כן ניתוסף להאדם, מתוך עטיו של נחש בירור חדש, שהוא כח הפועל השכלי, שאופני פעולתו ע"י על ידי בירורי אמת ושקר, שמוכרח לשמש עמו, בכל משך זמן מהלך התיקונים. שבלעדו הוא נמנע התועלת, כנ"ל באות ט"ז, עש"ה עיין שם היטב.

## "אכלתי ואוכל עוד"

(כא-7) ובוא והשכל כמות הבלבול שנתהוה, בסיבת נפילת הרפ"ח (288) ניצוצין לידי הס"א הסיטרא אחרא (הצד האחר), כי בטרם שטעמו מעץ הדעת, לא יכלה האשה, אף לנגוע בדבר האסור, כנ"ל באות י"ז, דאפי' שאפילו בקירוב נגיעה לעץ הדעת, תיכף טעמה, בו מרירות בטעם מות, דע"כ דעל כן הבינה והוסיפה, גם באיסור נגיעה, כנ"ל

even the prohibition against touching, as was mentioned above; see there. But after the first taste, when the operating system of the *Sitra Achra* and of falsehood prevailed in the existence of reality, then what had been prohibited to them [Adam and Eve] appeared to them to be so sweet in the beginning that they could no longer renounce it, as our sages said: "I have eaten, and I shall eat more," as was mentioned above (18-7).

## Correction in Times of Messiah

(21-8) By this, you will understand why the reward given for following the Holy Torah is defined only as giving peace to the body; it is because the entire purpose of the Torah is to bring about the Correction of the sin of the Tree of Knowledge, as the operating system of reality was confused by it. It is for this Correction that the Torah was given; that is, in order to elevate the 288 sparks back to [the System of] Holiness. Then the operating system of reality shall return to the Holiness and the confusion will be removed from the ways of existence of reality. As a result, people will be made fit on their own for their desired perfection by discerning between bitter and sweet alone, which was the first act [of Adam and Eve] before the sin of the Tree of Knowledge. And you [need to] understand it.

(21-9) The prophets, too, speak only about this Correction, which is why our sages said: "all the prophets had prophecies only about the Days of the Messiah," (*Bavli*, Tractate *Berachot* 34) which is all about bringing back the ways of existence of the world according to the refined Providence, as it was before the sin. "But as for the World to Come," (Ibid) namely, completing and achieving of Similarity of Form with the Creator, as discussed above, then "no eye has ever seen the Creator, except for You." (Ibid) Study that well. This is just as it was said about the Days of the Messiah: "If Egypt does not ascend, etc., the rain will not fall on them, etc.," (Zechariah 14:17) which refers to discerning between good and evil.

ע"ש עין שם, ואחר טעימה הא' שכבר שלטה הנהגת הס"א הצד האחר והשקר בקיום המציאות, נעשה להם האיסור כ"כ כל כך מתוק בתחילתו, עד שלא יכלו עוד לפרוש הימנו, כמ"ש כמה שכתבו [חכמינו] ז"ל, שאמר אכלתי ואוכל עוד כנ"ל (יח-7).

## תקון ימות משיח

(כא-8) ובזה תבין מה שהמתן שכר שבהתורה הק' הקדושה, מוגדר, רק בשלות הגופות, להיות, שכל ענין התורה, הוא להבאת תיקונו של חטא העצה"ד העץ הדעת, שנתבלבל ההנהגה של קיום המציאות על ידה. ולתיקון זה ניתנה התורה, כדי לחזור ולהעלות הרפ"ח (288) ניצוצין להקדושה, שאז ישוב ההנהגה של הקיום אל הקדושה, ויסורו הבלבולים, מדרכי הקיום המציאות, שאז יוכשרו בני אדם לשלימותם הנרצה, מאליהם, ע"י על ידי הבירור של מר ומתוק לבד, שהוא הפועל הראשון שבטרם חטאו של עצה"ד עץ הדעת, והבן.

(כא-9) וכן הנביאים, אינם מדברים אלא מתיקון הזה לבד, והיא שאמרו חז"ל (תלמוד בבלי, מסכת ברכות דף ל"ד): "כל הנביאים לא נתנבאו אלא לימות המשיח", שהוא ענין השבת דרכי קיום העולם בהשגחה המבוררת, כמו שהיתה קודם החטא, "אבל לעולם הבא", פי' פירוש גמר הענין שהוא השואת צורה ליוצרה כנ"ל, "עין לא ראתה אלהי"ם זולתיך", עש"ה עיין שם הכתוב, וכמו"ש וכמו שכתוב, שבימות המשיח, (אם) מצרים לא יעלה וכו' לא עליהם יהיה הגשם (זכריה יד' יז') וכו' והיינו ע"י על ידי בירור טו"ר טוב ורע כנ"ל.

# Chapter 22: A Tzadik Comes to the World

## Same Soul, Different Body

(22-1) Now we can understand the saying of our sages that we introduced [at the beginning of this book], that the Creator could not find a better fitting Vessel for containing a blessing for the Israelites other than peace, etc. (end of Tractate *Ukatzin*). We questioned why this phrase was chosen to end the *Talmud*. According to what has been said so far, it has been made clear that because of the sin of the Tree of Knowledge, the eternal Soul of Life, which the Creator blew into the nostrils of [Adam] was for his own needs, and [after the sin, it] received a new Form called the "sweat of life." This means that the whole [that is, the eternal soul] was divided into very many individual segments—into many tiny drops—which were divided between Adam, the First Man, and all his offspring, all the way to the end of time.

(22-2) Thus, there is no change at all in the act of the Creator except that there is an additional Form, for this general Light of Life, which was contained in the nostrils of Adam, the First Man, has been expanded to a great chain that reincarnates as a wheel of Difference of Form in many bodies, one body after another, until the necessary End of the *Tikkun* (Correction). And therefore, it happened that immediately upon eating from the Tree of Knowledge, [Adam and Eve] died and the Eternal Life left them and became attached to their reproductive organs (referring to mating, which is called *shalom* [peace], as was discussed in the *Zohar* and in the *Writings of the Ari*, Rav Isaac Luria), as has been said.

## We Create Immortality

(22-3) Therefore, it is clear that no person lives only for his own sake but rather for the sake of the whole chain and in such a way that each part of the chain does not receive the Light of Life into

# פרק כב: צדיק בא לעולם

## אותה נשמה, גוף אחר

(כב-1) **ועתה** מובן לנו מאמר חז"ל שנכנסנו בו, דלא מצא הקב"ה
הקדוש ברוך הוא כלי מחזיק ברכה לישראל אלא השלום וכו' (סוף מסכת
עוקצין), ועמדנו בו, למה נבחר מאמר זה לסיום הש"ס הששה סדרי משנה,
ומובן ע"פ על פי הנ"ל, דמסבת חטאו של עצה"ד עץ הדעת, פרח נשמת
חיים הנצחית, שנפח ה' באפו, לצרכי האדם הראשון לבדו, וקבלה
לצורה חדשה, המכונה זיעה של חיים, כלומר שנתחלק הכלל
לפרטים מרובים מאד, לטפין טפין, שנתחלק בין אה"ר אדם הראשון
וכל תולדותיו, עד עת קץ.

(כב-2) באופן, שאין שינוי כלל במעשה השי"ת השם יתברך אלא צורה
נוספה יש כאן, אשר זה אור החיים הכללי, שהיה צרורה באפו של
אה"ר אדם הראשון, נתפשט לשלשלת גדולה, המתגלגלת על גלגל
שינוי הצורה, בגופות מרובות, ובגוף אחר גוף, עד גמר התיקון
המחויב. ולפיכך נמצא שתיכף ביום אכילתו מעצה"ד מעץ הדעת מת,
ופרח הימנו חיים הנצחיים, אלא שנקשר באבר ההולדה, (שה"ע
שהוא ענין הזווג שנק' שנקרא שלום כמ"ש כמה שכתוב בזוהר וכהאר"י
ובכתבי האר"י) לשלשלת גדולה כאמור.

## אנחנו יוצרים נצחיות

(כב-3) ונמצא שאין אדם חי לצורך עצמו, אלא לצורך השלשלת
כולו, באופן שכל חלק וחלק מהשלשלת, אינו מקבל את אור החיים
לתוך עצמו, אלא רק משפיע אור החיים, לכללות השלשלת. וכן

itself, but only bestows the Light of Life upon the entirety of the chain. You find this in the calculation of the days of [a person's] life: When he is twenty, he is due to marry a woman, and then it is suitable to wait for ten years and then give birth to sons, as our sages said.

(22-4) And thus, in his thirties, he will surely have children. Then he sits and waits for his son [to grow] until he is forty—the age of understanding—so that he can pass on to [his son] all his wealth and knowledge that he has gained himself, as well as everything he has learnt and inherited from his ancestors. And he will then be sure that his son will not lose it in some evil venture. Then he immediately departs from this world and his son holds on to the rest of the chain, instead of his father.

## "He is Terrible in his Defaming of Human Beings"

(22-5) We have explained in verse 15 that the sin of the Tree of Knowledge was pre-ordained for Adam, the First Man. This is according to the verse: "He is terrible in his defaming of the children of man." (Psalms 66:5) Study that well. It is necessary [for a human being] to acquire, by building it, an external Vessel in order to receive the Surrounding Light in a manner where both opposites will be united in one retaining object (or carrier) during two periods of time, one after the other.

(22-6) During his *katnut* (smallness; also younger years), he is sustained by the *Sitra Achra* (Other Side), and through the fragmented source of pleasure that he receives from it, the Receiving Vessels of the Vacant Space grow in him, according to their desired dimensions. Then, by the time he reaches *gadlut* (magnitude; also maturity) and engages in the Torah and the Precepts, he will have the ability to alter these great Receiving Vessels [and transfom them to Receiving] for the Sake of Sharing. This is the main purpose, which is called both the Light of Truth and the seal, as was discussed earlier in verse 14; study that well.

אתה מוצא במדת ימי חייו, כי בעשרים שנה, ראוי לישא אשה. ועשר שנים, ראוי להמתין על לידת בנים, כמ"ש כמה שאמרו [חכמינו] ז"ל.

(כב-4) ונמצא מוליד בטוח, בשנת השלשים ואז, יושב וממתין על בנו, עד שיגיע לארבעים שנה, ימי בינה, באופן, שיוכל למסור לו, את ההון וידיעותיו, שרכש בעצמו, וכל אשר למד וירש מאבותיו, ויהיה בטוח עליו, שלא יאבד זה בענין רע, שאז תיכף הולך לו לעולמו, ובנו נאחז בהמשך השלשלת, תחת אביו.

## "נורא עלילה לבני אדם"

(כב-5) **והנה** נתבאר לעיל אות ט"ו, אשר מקרה החטא של עצה"ד עץ הדעת, היה במחוייב לאה"ר לאדם הראשון, בסו"ה בסוד הכתוב נורא עלילה לבני האדם (תהילים סו, ה), עש"ה עיין שם הכתוב. כי צריך לקנות בבנינו, כלי חצון, לקבלת אור מקיף, באופן, שב' ההפכים יבואו בנושא אחד, בב' זמנים בזה אחר זה.

(כב-6) שבזמן קטנותו, יהיה סמוך על שלחן הס"א הסיטרא אחרא (הצד האחר), וע"י ועל ידי התענוגים דפרודא שמקבל בחמתם, מתגדלים בו הכלי קבלה דחלל הפנוי, בשיעורם הנרצה, ואז, כשמגיע לגדלותו, ועוסק בתורה ומצות, יהיה מצוי לו היכולת, להפוך כלי קבלה הגדולים, בע"מ בעל מנת להשפיע שהיא עיקר המטרה, שנקרא שנק' אור האמת, והחותם, כנ"ל באות י"ד עש"ה עיין שם היטב.

## A *Tzadik* (Righteous Person) in Every Generation

(22-7) Indeed, it is known that before connecting to the [System of] Holiness, [a person] has to detach from all the Forms of Receiving that he has acquired from the table of the *Sitra Achra* (Other Side), just as the Precept of Love has come to us "with all your soul and with all your might." (Deuteronomy 6:5) So now what good did the sages do by establishing the laws if a person goes back and loses again all that he has gained from the *Sitra Achra*. Contemplate this well. Therefore, the Providence [of the Creator] has prepared an increasing number of bodies in each and every generation, to such an extent that our sages have said, "He realized that the *tzadikim* (righteous) are but a few, so He planted them in each and every generation." (Tractate *Yoma* 38b).

(22-8) This means that [the Creator] saw that the righteous are bound to completely reject the idea of Receiving for the Self Alone and that their Surrounding Light would thereby diminish, since the external Vessel that is fit for it was rejected away from them. Therefore, He planted the *tzadikim* (righteous people) in each and every generation because every generation has a large percentage of people who are created mainly for the sake of the righteous and who are the carriers of the Vessels of the Vacant Space for [the righteous]. In this way, the external Vessel is used for the righteous by [the rest of the people], although by coercion and not voluntarily.

(22-9) This is because all the [earthly] inhabitants are attached to each other; they interact with each other and influence each other in terms of both bodily tendencies and opinions. Therefore, they automatically bring the tendencies of selfish receiving to the righteous, and so in this manner, [the righteous] are able to receive the desired Surrounding Light. According to this, however, the righteous and the wicked would have to be in equal [numbers] in each generation, but this is not so. Rather, for every single righteous person, we find thousands upon thousands of shallow people.

## צדיק בכל דור

(כב-7) אמנם נודע, שבטרם שמתחבר להקדושה, מחוייב שוב להתפרש, מכל צורת הקבלה, שהשיג משולחן הס"א הסיטרא אחרא (הצד האחר) כמו שהגיע אלינו מצוות האהבה, בכל נפשך ובכל מאודך (דברים, ו', ה'), וא"כ ואם כן מה הועילו חכמים בתקנתם, דשוב חזר ואבד, כל מה שהשיג מס"א מסיטרא אחרא (מהצד האחר), ודו"ק ודייק היטב. ולפיכך, הזמין השגחתו ית' יתברך, ריבוי הגופות בכל דור ודור, עד שאמרו [חכמינו] ז"ל, ראה הצדיקים שהמה מועטים, עמד ושתלן בכל דור ודור (מסכת יומא דף לח', עמוד ב').

(כב-8) פי' פירוש, שראה [הבורא] ית' יתברך, שסופם של הצדיקים, לדחות לגמרי ענין הקבלה העצמיית, ונמצאים נתמעטים מאור מקיף שלהם, כי נדחה מהם כלי החצון הראוי לזה, וע"כ ועל כן שתלן בכל דור ודור, שאין לך דור שלא יהיה בו חלק גדול מאותם הבריות שעיקר בריאתם אינם אלא בשביל הצדיקים, שיהיו המה הנושאים בחי' בחינת הכלים דחלל הפנוי, בשבילם שיתפעל בהצדיקים בחי' בחינת כלי חיצון על ידיהם, על צד ההכרח שלא ברצונם.

(כב-9) והוא, מפני שכל בני הישוב, יש להם דביקות זה עם זה, להתפעל זה מזה, הן בנטיות הגוף, והן בדעות, וע"כ ועל כן, המה מביאים במחוייב, את נטיות הקבלה עצמיית, להצדיקים, שבאופן זה מסוגלים לקבל, את האור מקיף הנרצה. אמנם לפי"ז לפי זה, היו צריכים צדיקים ורשעים להמצא בכל דור ודור במשקל השוה, ואינו כן, אלא על צדיק אחד, אנו מוצאים אלפי רבבות של ריקים.

## Qualitative and Quantitative Power

(22-10) You should know, however, that there [we] can find two kinds of dominance over Creation: One is a qualitative power, and the second is a quantitative power. All those who conduct their lives in accordance with the *Sitra Achra* (Other Side), their power is weak, pathetic, despicable, and low, without will and without purpose; they are pushed back like straw tossed by the wind. This being so, how could such people have any influence among people of wisdom—whose ways are chosen with motivation and purpose and for whom the column of the Supernal Light shines upon their path day and night—and to such an extent that they are able to bring their tiny inclinations into their hearts. For this reason, the Creator introduced into Creation the quantitative force because this force does not need quality at all.

(22-11) I will explain [this concept] to you in the the following way: We find a qualitative force in heroism, like with lions and tigers where no man would fight against them because of the great quality of the might of their heroism. In contrast, we find [instances of] might and heroism without any quality at all, only quantity, as in the case of flies, which no man would attempt to fight against because of their sheer quantity, with the result that these pests have total freedom in a man's house and on his set table, while he feels weak in front of them.

(22-12) This is not the case when it comes to the insects of the field [and] reptiles and their like, in terms of unwanted guests. Even though their power is of higher quality than that of the house flies, a man would not stand still or rest until he manages to completely chase them away from his surroundings. This is because nature has not granted them the power of great numbers as it has with the flies. Through this, you will understand that there has to be a very large multitude of people for each and every *tzadik* (righteous person) for them to be able to effect their crude tendencies on him; [they can do this only] through their power of quantity because they have no quality whatsoever. Understand this well, and this is not the place to go into it at length.

## כוח איכותי וכוח כמותי

(כב-10) אלא צריך שתדע ב' מיני שליטות, הנמצאים בהבריאה. הא', הוא כח איכותי, הב', הוא כח כמותי. ולהיות שכל אותם המתנהלים לרגלי הס"א הסיטרא אחרא (הצד האחר), כחם דל ומצער בזוי ושפל, בלי חפץ ובלי מטרה, אלא הולכין ונהדפים כמוץ לפני רוח. א"כ אם כן, איך יוכלו כאלה, לפעול מה, באנשים חכמי לב, שדרכיהם מבורר בחפץ ותכלית, ועמוד אור העליון מאיר לפניהם יומם ולילה. באופן, שיספיקו להביא נטיותיהם הקטנטנות בלבבם. אשר ע"כ על כן, הזמין [הבורא] ית' יתברך, כח הכמותי בהבריאה, שכח הזה, אינו צריך לאיכות של כלום.

(כב-11) ואסביר לך, על דרך שאנו מוצאים, כח האיכותי בגבורה כמו באריות ונמרים. אשר מרוב האיכות שבכח גבורתם, שום אדם לא ילחם בהם. ולעומתם, אנו מוצאים כח וגבורה, בלו איכות של כלום, אלא בכמות לבד, כמו הזבובים. שלגודל הריבוי שבהם, שום אדם לא ילחום עמהם, וטיילים האלו, בני חורין המה בביתו של אדם, ועל שולחנו הערוך, והאדם מרגיש את עצמו חלש לנגדם.

(כב-12) משא"כ מה שאין כן, לעומת זבובי השדה, ושרצים, וכדומה, מאורחים בלתי קרואים, הגם שכחם יהיה ביתר איכות מזבובים הביתים, לא ישקוט האדם, ולא ינוח, עד כלה יגרש אותם מרשותו. והוא, מפני שהטבע לא הנחיל להם כח הריבוי, כמו לזבובים. וע"פ ועל פי זה תבין, אשר בהכרח, מחוייב להמצא המון גדול מאוד, על כל צדיק וצדיק, עדי שיפעלו בו את נטיותיהם הגסות, בכח הריבוי שבהם, משום שאין להם איכות של כלום, והבן היטב, ואכמ"ל ואין כאן מה להאריך עוד.

# Chapter 23: Peace is a Fitting Vessel to Contain Blessing

## The Creator's Guarantee for Immortality

(23-1) And this is what is meant by the passage: "May the Creator give strength to his people." (Psalms 29:11) It means that the eternal Light of Life, which is attained by all the chain of creation, is called "strength"[Heb. *oz*]. And the Scripture promises us that the Creator gives us this strength with certainty. Indeed, we should ask, how so? The reason is that each of us is not a complete entity unto himself, as our sages have said, "It would have been better for mankind not to have been created than to have been created," (Tractate *Eruvin*, 13b) and therefore, how can we be certain of the eternity of the [Light of Life]?

(23-2) That is why the Psalm ends with: "May the Creator bless his people with *shalom* (peace)." (Psalms 29:11) This alludes to the blessing of having sons and is in accord with what the sages said in Tractate *Shabbat* (152a): "[The *Shabbat*] introduces peace in the house of the idle" because through the sons, the chain is extended and continues all the way to the End of the *Tikkun* (Correction). And then all the parts are in a state of eternity." Understand this, although here is not the place to go into it at length.

## Fathers, Sons, and the Blessing of Immortality

(23-3) Therefore, our sages said that the Creator did not find a Vessel other than peace to contain His blessing for the Israelites (end of Tractate *Ukatzin*) because just as His blessing is eternal, the recipients must also be eternal. Thus we conclude that the fathers hold on to their sons, and they create between them a chain of eternity that is worthy of holding the blessing of eternity. Hence, peace is what contains and presides over the completion of the blessing.

# פרק כג: השלום- כלי מחזיק ברכה

## הבטחת הבורא לחיים נצחיים

(כג-1) וזה שיעור הכתוב, ה' עוז לעמו יתן (תהילים כט, יא), פי' פירוש, שאור החיים הנצחי, המושג לכל שלשלת הבריאה, הוא נקרא עוז, ומבטיח לנו הכתוב, שהשי"ת שהשם יתברך נותן לנו בבטחה העוז הזה. אמנם יש להקשות הא כיצד, כיון דכל אחד ואחד, אינו ענין שלם לעצמו, כמ"ש כמו שאמרו [חכמינו] ז"ל, (מסכת עירובין דף יג', עמוד ב') "טוב לו לאדם שלא נברא משנברא" וא"כ ואם כן, איך אנו בטוחים בנצחיותו ית' יתברך.

(כג-2) וזה שגומר הכתוב, ה' יברך את עמו בשלום (תהילים כט, יא), והיינו, ברכת הבנים, ע"ד על דרך שאמרו [חכמינו] ז"ל, במסכת שבת (דף קנב', עמוד א') משים שלום בבית בטל, כי ע"י על ידי הבנים, נמשך ונקשר השלשלת הזה עד גמר התיקון, ואז נמצאים כל החלקים בנצחיות, ואכמ"ל ואין כאן מקום להאריך והבן.

## אבות, בנים וברכת הנצחיות

(כג-3) ולפכיך, אמרו [חכמינו] ז"ל, לא מצא הקב"ה הקדוש ברוך הוא כלי מחזיק ברכה לישראל אלא השלום (מסכת עוקצין, דף אחרון), כי כמו שברכתו ית' היא נצחיית, צריכים המקבלים ג"כ גם כן להיות נצחיים, ובזה נמצא אשר ע"י על ידי הבנים, נאחזים האבות, ועושים בינהם שלשלת הנצחיות, הראוי להחזיק ברכה הנצחיות, ונמצא שהשלום הוא המחזיק ומנצח על שלימות הברכה.

157

(22-16) Therefore, [our sages] concluded the *Shas* (the "six orders" of the *Mishnah*) with this saying because peace, as mentioned above (22-14), is the Vessel that holds for us the blessing of the Torah and all the Precepts, up until the complete and eternal Redemption— may it come rapidly in our days. And everything will reach its ultimate purpose in peace.

(כג-4) ולפיכך סיימו סיימו הש"ס הששה סידרי משנה במאמר הזה, להיות
השלום כנ"ל (כג-2), הוא הכלי מחזיק בעדינו ברכת התורה וכל
המצוות, עד לגאולה שלימה ולנצחיות, בבי"א במהרה בימינו אמן, והכל
על מקומו יבוא בשלום.

# *Glossary*

**320 (*Shach*)** – A term that refers to the 320 sparks of Light that fell into the void as a result of the Shattering of the Vessels. Thirty-two (*Lev*) of these 320 sparks are "trapped" in a place where we are not able to correct them until the time of the final phase of the Correction (*Tikkun*); this leaves 288 sparks to do the job. The 32 trapped sparks are also called *Lev haEven* (Heart Made of Stone). See also: **Shattering of the Vessels, *Tikkun***

**288 (*Rapach*)** – Refers to the 288 sparks of Light that constitute the souls of all humanity that come into this world to make the correction through positive consciousness and actions. These 288 sparks are the source that feeds the reality of Good and Evil and they form the foundation for the World of *Tikkun* (Correction). See also: ***Tikkun***

**613** – The number of Precepts or spiritual guidelines that strengthen our spiritual and physical relationship with our fellowman and the Creator. All these Precepts can be found within the *Five Books of Moses*. The Precepts are separated into two categories: 248 Precepts of proactive/positive "do" actions that help us remove obstacles in our spiritual path and give us clarity, and 365 Precepts of reactive/negative "do not do" actions. Performing both types of Precepts will bring us closer to the Creator.

**Abraham the Patriarch** – An important figure in the *Book of Genesis*, Abraham is one of the three patriarchs of the Torah and the father of Isaac the Patriarch. Abraham's life and actions were the epitome of absolute sharing. Abraham is a chariot and the link to the *Sefira* of *Chesed* (Mercy). Connecting to him gives us the energy of mercy and unconditional sharing. See also: **Chariot, Ten *Sefirot***

**Act of Creation *(Ma'aseh Beresheet)*** – A concept referring both to the creation of the world in six days, as described in the *Book* *of Genesis*, and to the *Study of the Ten Luminous Emanations*. The greatest kabbalists were able to tap into *Ma'aseh Beresheet* and could perform miracles for others in need, miracles that defied the laws of nature that were established in the moment of Creation. *Ma'aseh Beresheet* is taught to one student at a time in one-on-one study, and only few select students in each generation have the merit of achieving this level.

**Act of the Chariot *(Ma'aseh Merkavah)* –** The study of the *Merkavah* (Chariot or Assembling) is a deep, secret kabbalistic study that refers to the structure and hierarchy of the Upper Worlds. Being a study above and beyond logic, *Ma'aseh Merkavah* is a level of consciousness that should be studied by a qualified kabbalist on his own.

**Angels –** Frequencies or packets of spiritual energy intelligence that constantly roam and move about among us, acting as messengers from the Creator and affecting things that happen in our daily life. We can imagine an angel as being a conduit or channel that transports cosmic energy or thoughts from one place to another or from one spiritual dimension to the other. Angels have no free will, and each angel is dedicated to one specific purpose. See also: **Free will**

**Animal Kingdom –** The third of the Four Kingdoms (Inanimate, Vegetative, Animal, Speaking), with a larger capacity of Desire to Receive than either the Inanimate or Vegetative Kingdoms, but less of a capacity than the Speaking Kingdom. See also: **Inanimate Kingdom, Speaking Kingdom, Vegetative Kingdom**

**Ari –** Rav Isaac Luria, often called "the Ari" or "the Holy Lion." Born in 1534 in Jerusalem, he died in 1572 in the city of Safed in the Galilee region of Israel. Considered to be the father of contemporary Kabbalah, the Ari was a foremost kabbalistic scholar and the founder of the Lurianic method of learning and teaching Kabbalah. His closest student, Rav Chaim Vital, compiled and wrote the Ari's teachings word for word in 18 volumes. These 18 volumes are collectively known as *Kitvei haAri* or the *Writings of the Ari*. See also: **Rav Chaim Vital**

*Asiyah* – See: **World of Action**

*Atzilut* – See: **World of Emanation**

**Baal Shem Tov** – Rav Israel, the "Master of the Good Name" (1690–1760) was an important kabbalist from Ukraine and the founder of the Chasidic movement. While the Baal Shem Tov himself did not write any books, his teachings have been disseminated through the many Chasidic books and articles that were written in his name. Hundreds of great kabbalists and *tzadikim* (righteous people) through the ages, including The Kabbalah Center today, have followed and applied his system.

**Ben Zoma** – A kabbalistic sage of the *Mishnah* and one of four spiritual giants—Ben Zoma, Ben Azai, Akher, and Rav Akiva—who entered the *PaRDeS* (literally "orchard") to bring an end to pain and suffering in the world by using the secrets of the Kabbalah and the Torah.

*Beriah* – See: **World of Creation**

**Book of Formation** (*Sefer Yetzirah*) – The earliest known book of kabbalistic knowledge and wisdom. Written by Abraham the Patriarch some 3800 years ago, it deals primarily with the intrinsic power within the Aramaic-Hebrew letters and the stars, and how both the letters and stars affect us in this world. All the secrets of Creation that will eventually be revealed are considered to be concealed in this book.

**Chariot** – A chariot is like the saddle on a horse, which connects the rider and the horse. Chariots help us to connect to the Upper Worlds. The Patriarchs, along with Moses, Aaron, Joseph the Righteous, and King David are all considered chariots for the Lower

Seven *Sefirot*. When we connect to a specific chariot, we elevate our consciousness and give ourselves a spiritual boost.

**Cleaving** (*Devekut*) – A concept describing how close we should be to the Creator. We need to "cleave" and be as one with the Creator. Proximity in the spiritual world is measured not by space or distance but by the degree of similarity that exists between the two entities, which is known in Kabbalah as Similarity of Form. The closer we are to behaving like the Creator, the closer we get to becoming like God. When we act selfishly, reactively, and negatively, we distance ourselves from the Creator and are not cleaving to Him. When we act selflessly, like the Creator, we become closer to Him. In other words, the more we become like God, the more *Devekut* (Cleaving) we have with Him. See also: **Difference of Form, Similarity of Form**

**Concealed Torah** (*Sitrei* **Torah**)–Aspects of the Torah whose meaning is hidden (also called the Secrets of the Torah or *Sitrei* Torah). Concealed Torah is essentially a reference to the Wisdom of Kabbalah. One reason that Kabbalah is referred to as the Concealed Torah is because Kabbalah is concealed from the immediate and literal understanding of the Torah. Another reason is that the Creator is concealing Himself in the Torah. To access the Concealed Torah, one needs a certain level of purity, a positive way of conduct, and a master kabbalist as a guide. See: **Revealed Torah,** *Ta'amei* **Torah**

**Contraction** – See: *Tzimtzum*

**Correction** – See: *Tikkun*

**Creator** – The Endless Light or the Lightforce of God; the Cause of all Causes.

**Days of Messiah** – The era of Redemption sometime in the future, when exile and slavery, both spiritual and physical, will end. According to the *Talmud*, during this time, the Third Temple will be built and many will come to Jerusalem from the four corners of the world. According to Kabbalah, this will be a time of awareness and transformation when people will be free from their selfish needs and will easily express their true nature, that of sharing. See also: **End of** *Tikkun,* *Tikkun*

*Derash* – The third level of the *PaRDeS,* and one of the four ways to interpret every word and sentence in the Torah. *Derash* is the underlying understanding of the lessons from each section of the Torah that we can apply in our daily life. *Derash* is the homiletic exposition in contrast to *Peshat,* the literal interpretation. See also: **PaRDeS**

**Difference of Form** – The opposite of Similarity of Form. The essence or form of the Creator is one of sharing. According to the Law of Attraction, when we do not share and instead act selfishly, we are in Difference of Form with the Creator, with the result that we are not cleaving to Him, but distancing ourselves from Him. See also: **Cleaving, Similarity of Form**

**Empty Space** – A concept taught in the *Study of the Ten Luminous Emanations.* It is a metaphysical place where the Light of the Creator is not revealed. Thus the space appears as if it is empty of Light.

**End of the** *Tikkun* – The time when we, as a collective, have transformed our nature and have become completely sharing beings. When we are in true Similarity or Affinity of Form with the Creator, we will have reached the End of the *Tikkun* (literally, the Fixing or the Correction) and the Days of Messiah will arrive. See also: **Days of Messiah, Similarity of Form,** *Tikkun*

*Etz HaChayim (Tree of Life)* – The first four volumes in the 18-volume set of the *Writings of the Ari,* written by Rav Isaac Luria (the Ari). They contain the main teachings of the *Study of Ten Luminous Emanations.*

**Evil Inclination** – Each of us always has two inner voices that guide us to do everything, whether positive (proactive) or negative (reactive). The Evil Inclination is the voice that pushes us to be reactive and negative. It is sometimes referred to as Satan, which in Hebrew simply means "Adversary." The Evil Inclination is our internal opponent that always tells us to act selfishly and reactively.

**Free will** – A concept found in all religions and philosophies. The kabbalists say that we have free will so that we can transform our Desire to Receive for the Self Alone to the Desire to Receive for the Sake of Sharing.

*Geonim* (plural of *Gaon*) – Kabbalists living during the 6th to 11th centuries CE who were the presidents of the two great Babylonian Talmudic academies, *Sura* and *Pumbedita*, as well as the Talmudic academy of Israel. They were the only ones in their respective generations who had access to the *Zohar*. Their position was incumbent on their ability to grasp the knowledge they received from the scholars in the generations prior to their own.

*Halachah* – Any spiritual law of the universe that is based on the 613 Precepts. The later Talmudic laws along with customs and traditions are collectively referred to as *Halachah*. The literal meaning of *Halachah* is "the path" because *Halachah* is a way of connecting to the path of life through the actions that we do. For those who want to follow a spiritual quest, *Halachah* is a system of instructions for what to do, how, and when. See also: **613**

**He and His Name Are One** – A kabbalistic concept referring to the reality that existed before the *Tzimtzum* (Contraction). "He" refers to the Light of the Creator; "His Name" refers to the Vessel. There was no distinction or separation between the Light and the Vessel in the reality before the *Tzimtzum*. See also: **Shattering of the Vessels**, *Tzimtzum*

*Idra Zuta* (**Small Assembly**) – A section of the *Zohar* that appears in the portion of *Ha'azinu*. The *Idra Zuta* teaches the secrets that Rav Shimon bar Yochai revealed to his son and his five other students on the day of his passing.

**Inanimate Kingdom** – Of the Four Kingdoms (Inanimate, Vegetative, Animal, Speaking), this is the lowest level, representing the lowest intensity of the Desire to Receive. See also: **Animal Kingdom, Speaking Kingdom, Vegetative Kingdom**

**Introduction to the Gates** – Eight books from the *Writings of the Ari*. These *Eight Gates* (*Shemona Shearim*) are the wisdom Rav Chaim Vital was taught by the Ari and that he later compiled into books.

**Isaac the Patriarch** – One of the three patriarchs of the Torah, Isaac was the son of Abraham and the father of Jacob. We learn about the spirit of Isaac from the biblical story of the Binding of Isaac where he showed courage and completely let go of his personal agenda. Isaac is a chariot for the *Sefira* of *Gevurah*. Connecting with him can give us the courage and ability to overcome challenges and hardship. See also: **Ten *Sefirot***

**Israelite** – A code name for anyone following a spiritual path and working on his or her negative traits, and constantly striving to transform them to positive ones. Israelites are people who take upon themselves the responsibility of spreading the Light and for putting other people's needs before their own. They also understand and follow the spiritual rules of cause and effect, and do not take the Torah literally but rather as a coded message.

**Jacob the Patriarch** – One of the three patriarchs of the Torah, Jacob was the son of Isaac and the father of the 12 tribes of Israel. Having to hide away from his brother for 20 years and facing other grave challenges for most of his life, Jacob lived a life of restriction. Nevertheless, he kept absolute trust in the Creator and therefore never disconnected from the Light of the Creator. Jacob is a chariot and a link to the *Sefira* of *Tiferet*, which represents balance and absolute certainty. See also: **Ten *Sefirot***

*Klippot* – See: **Shells**

*Komah* – Literally "stature" or "tallness," *komah* is the total number of levels within a spiritual or physical Vessel. The *komah* measures the "size" of the Vessel. See also: **Vessel**

**Light of Endless** – The Light of the Creator, which is the living essence of everything in the physical and spiritual universe. Light of Endless indicates that in this realm where the Light of the Creator is revealed in its raw, naked form, there is no end, limitation, or chaos of any sort. The Light of Endless is the total energy that is received in the Worlds. It is everything except the Vessels (i.e., everything except the Desire to Receive).

*Midrash* **(Study)** – A method of interpreting the Bible, incorporating stories and tales, going deeper than the conventional commentaries. The *Midrash* consists of stories that touch mostly the essence and spirit of the study as well as some concealed secrets.

*Midrash haNe'elam* (*The Concealed Study*) – A book that is a part of *Zohar Chadash* (*New Zohar*). It was written by Rav Shimon bar Yochai just as the *Zohar* and the *Zohar Chadash* were, and is a partial commentary on the Torah and additional Scrolls. See also: *Zohar*

*Midrash Rabbah* – Literally "the great study or essay," this is the complete collection of the *Midrash*—explanations and more detailed accounts, poetic reflections, and homilies—on each of the *Five Books of Moses*.

**Mouth-to-Ear Kabbalah** – Study of the Wisdom of Kabbalah from the mouth of the teacher to the ear of the student who receives his knowledge by listening to his teacher and reading written material. Through this system, the student receives the knowledge of his teacher.

**Mouth-to-Mouth Kabbalah** – Study of the Wisdom of Kabbalah from the mouth of the kabbalistic master directly to the mouth of the student. The student receives the thoughts and consciousness of his teacher, including secrets and ideas that are not available in books.

*Neshama* (**Soul**) – A spark of the Creator that was put in the physical body to allow its spiritual work and growth, so that the individual can excel, become like God, and cleave to the Creator.

*Or Pnimi* (**Inner Light**) – The Light that we have earned through our proactive actions. This Light is who we are and what we are; it is our life experience and wisdom. See: **Surrounding** Light

*Or Makif* (**Surrounding Light**) – The Light that pushes us to grow and reveal our potential Light. *Or Makif* refers to our potential and to everything we were meant to accomplish throughout our lifetime. *Or Makif* is connected to the quantum Light of the Creator, that waits to be revealed through our proactive actions.

*Or Yashar* (**Straight Light**) – The Light of the Creator before it has any interaction with a vessel. *Or Yashar* is Light in its raw, naked form, it has no manifestation as yet. See also: **Vessel**

*Or Chozer* (**Returning Light**) – The Light that bounces back from the spiritual vessel that is not ready to receive it. Our spiritual vessel was designed to receive the Light of the Creator and manifest the good concealed in it. A part of the vessel that is not yet ready for the Light pushes the Light back. See also: **Vessel**

*PaRDeS* –Literally meaning "orchard," *PaRDeS* is an acronym of the initial letters of the four words that refer to the four levels of study and understanding of the Bible: *Peshat, Remez, Derash,* and *Sod.* Every word and letter in the Torah can be understood in four different ways: *Peshat,* the simple and literal meaning; *Remez,* the allegorical meaning behind the word, metaphors that stand for a higher meaning; *Derash,* the in-depth explanation and homiletical meanings; and *Sod,* the secrets behind the words, where the Wisdom of Kabbalah comes from.

*Partzuf* (Face) – A whole and complete spiritual structure of the Ten *Sefirot. Partzuf* represents the Head—the Upper Three *Sefirot*—or potential, and the Body—the Lower Seven *Sefirot*—or actual. There are five *Partzufim* (plural of *Partzuf*) in the metaphysical world: *Arich Anpin* (Long Face), *Aba* (Father), *Ima* (Mother), *Zeir Anpin* (Small Face), *Nukvah* (Female). See also: **Ten *Sefirot***

**Patriarchs** – Abraham, Isaac, and Jacob, who are the three pillars of the Torah. They are referred to as the chariots and channels for the *Sefirot* of *Chesed* (Right column), *Gevurah* (Left column), and *Tiferet* (Central columns) that we can use to achieve balance in our day-to-day life. See also: **Ten *Sefirot***

*Penimiyut* (Inner part of the Torah) – The hidden meaning and essence that is concealed within the text of the Torah. It is the source of life for those who merit connecting to it. The external part of the Torah is the literal understanding and the stories of the Torah.

*Peshat* – The simple meaning behind the words of the Torah and a literal interpretation of its stories and events. *Peshat* is considered the cornerstone for the other three ways of understanding the Torah. See also: *PaRDeS*

**Precepts** – See: **613**

*Pri Etz Chaim* (*The Fruit of the Tree of Life*) – A book that was written originally by Rav Chaim Vital from the teachings he heard from the Ari. Today, it is in two volumes, printed as a part of the 18-volume set of the *Writings of the Ari. Pri Etz Chaim* teaches the meditations for the prayers and precepts of the different cosmic events of the year.

**Prophets** – Men or women who were so connected to God that they could speak with Him, either directly, through an additional medium, or in dreams. These prophets were the connection between the Israelites and God. Nowadays, the only prophecies that exist are through our dreams, although because of our ego and selfish desires, these dreams often get muddled and their true meaning is lost or misconstrued.

**Providence** – Everything that happens on this Earth is led by Divine Providence. The *Zohar* tells us that even every single blade of grass has its own individual angel that tells it to grow. In short, every action or event happens with the express oversight of the Creator Himself, and no matter how bad things may seem to us, the Light of Creator is there.

**Ramak** – Acronym for Rav Moshe Cordoveiro (1522–1570), one of the most important kabbalists and a spiritual leader of Safed in Israel in the 16th century. The Ramak was the teacher for a short time of Rav Isaac Luria (the Ari).

**Rav Abraham Azulai** – A kabbalist from Morocco (1570–1643) and student of Rav Chaim Vital and his son Rav Shmuel Vital. Rav Azulai wrote commentaries on the *Zohar*, the Bible, and other kabbalistic books, revealing the secrets of immortality.

**Rav Abraham Ibn Ezra** – A kabbalist, philosopher, poet, mathematician, astronomer and astrologer from Spain (1089–1164). Ibn Ezra wrote a commentary on a large part of the Bible as well as books on astronomy and astrology.

**Rav Chaim Vital** – The closest and greatest student of the Ari. Blessed with an incredible memory, he was able to write down everything the Ari taught him during the two years they were together before the Ari passed away, resulting in the 18-volume set of the *Writings of the Ari*.

**Rav Meir Paprish** – A kabbalist from Poland (1624–1662) and a student of Rav Yaakov Tzemach. After traveling to Damascus and reading the writings of Rav Shmuel Vital, he then decided to edit the *Writings of the Ari* into three books: *Etz Chaim*, *Pri Etz Chaim* and *Nof Etz Chaim*. Rav Meir wrote 39 books altogether, but not all were printed.

**Rav Moshe Botarel** – A Spanish kabbalist of the late 14th/early 15th centuries. Rav Moshe is famous for his commentary on the *Book of Formation (Sefer Yetzirah)*. See also: *Book of Formation*

**Rav Shmuel Vital** – A kabbalist from Damascus, Syria (1598–1677) and the son of Rav Chaim Vital. He redacted his father's compilation of the Ari's teachings to become the *Writings of the Ari* that we know today. The most reliable source for the writings of his father, Rav Shmuel himself wrote many books, although most were never published. Among his published books are the famous *Eight Gates*, eight volumes that are the most inclusive compiled text we have today of the words of the Ari. See also: *Introduction to the Gates*

**Rav Yaakov Tzemach** – A kabbalist and doctor from Portugal (1570–1667) and a student of Rav Shmuel Vital. Both teacher and student, together with Rav Abraham Azulai, went to the resting place of Rav Chaim Vital, and through special prayers and connections, Rav Chaim Vital revealed himself and gave them permission—years after his passing—to take his writings from their hiding place, compile them, and publish them.

**Remez (Hint or Clue)** – The second level of the *PaRDeS*, *Remez* is the hidden meaning behind the words in the Torah. See also: *PaRDeS*

**Revealed Torah** – The simple literal meaning of the written Torah, *Mishnah*, and *Talmud*. See also: **Concealed Torah**

**Righteous (*Tzadik*)** – A person who is completely devoted to working on transforming his or her negative traits and to sharing unconditionally with others. The *Midrash* also tells us that this is a person whose positive actions outweigh his or her negative actions.

**Rishonim (Firsts)** – The great commentators on the *Mishnah* and *Talmud* who lived between the 11th and 15th centuries CE. Among the most prominent *Rishonim* are *Rashi* and the sages who wrote the *Tosefot*. See also: *Tosefot*

**Sages** – Kabbalists from the time of the Second Temple who were very wise individuals that left us with deep wisdom and many lessons found in the *Mishnah* and *Talmud*.

*Sefirot* - see **Ten *Sefirot*, *Tet Sefirot***

*Shas* – An acronym for the Hebrew words *Shisha Sedarim*, the six orders of the *Mishnah*. The *Shas* is the first part of the oral Torah, which was given to Moses on Mount Sinai but which did not include the written *Torah* (i.e., the *Five Books of Moses*). Each one of the six orders of the *Mishnah* consists of various tractates that teach moral conduct pertaining to various areas of our life. The *Mishnah* was composed by the *Tanna'im*, kabbalists living in Israel between the years 180 BCE and 200 CE. See also: **Tractate and Entries For Individual Tractates**

**Shattering of the Vessels**– An event that took place before Creation when the spiritual Vessels shattered as result of a surge of Light from the Creator that they could not handle and contain. The sparks of Light from this shattering fell into the Lower Levels and were covered by the *klipot* (literally "veils": the negative entities that cover the Light of the Creator just as the skin of a fruit covers the fruit). The Shattering of the Vessels gave way to a new reality, where the Vessels were given the choice, through the process of *Tikkun*, to determine the amount of Light they wanted to contain.

*Shechinah* (**Divine Presence**) – The Light of the Creator when it is on its closest frequency to the physical world. The *Shechinah* is also the collective soul of all Israelites. The *Shechinah* corresponds to the female aspect of the Light of the Creator, and many writings refer to the union between God and the *Shechinah*. In addition, the *Shechinah* is a protection division of the Creator for the all those who connect to the Tree of Life.

**Shells (*Klipot; singular Klipa*)** – Evil husks created by mankind's negative deeds, they are the metaphysical negative covering that hides the Light of the Creator from us and gives it to the Negative

Side. These *klipot* also latch on to the sparks of Light we do not reveal when we fail to act on a positive impulse or action, or when we perform a selfish or negative action. See also: **Shattering of the Vessels**

*Shir haYichud* (The Song of Unification) – A song that was written by a kabbalist from the 12th or 13th century, although it is not certain which kabbalist actually wrote it. The *Shir haYichud* contains seven verses for the seven days of the week. In many congregations today, it is read, in different ways, as a part of the *Shabbat* meditation.

*Shlach Lecha* – The fourth portion in the *Book of Numbers*. *Shalach Lecha* is best known for its story about the journey of and its consequences for the 12 spies (the heads of the 12 Tribes) whom Moses sent to explore the Land of Canaan (Israel).

**Similarity of Form** – The state of being like the Creator. The Creator is a completely sharing Being. That is His Form. When we act selflessly and do not succumb to the Desire to Receive for the Self Alone, we are in Similarity of Form with the Creator. We are cleaving to Him, getting closer to His Supernal splendor. See also: *Cleaving, Difference of Form*

*Sitra Achra* (**Other Side**) – According to Kabbalah, the world is made of opposites: positive and negative, good and evil. The Light of the Creator represents the side of positivity, order, and clarity, while the *Sitra Achra* (Other Side) represents negativity, darkness, and chaos. The *Sitra Achra* needs a source of energy but cannot feed directly from the Light of the Creator. Every time we make a wrong choice or get upset and act reactively, the *Sitra Achra* can take advantage of this and suck the Light away from us.

*Sod* – The fourth level of the *PaRDeS* (i.e., the four ways to interpret every word and sentence in the Torah). *Sod* is the Secrets of the Torah, the Wisdom of Kabbalah. Studying the *Sod* requires a high level of purity of the body and mind and is taught one-on-one by a master kabbalist to his student. See also: *PaRDeS*

**Speaking Kingdom** – The highest level of consciousness and Desire to Receive of the Four Kingdoms (Inanimate, Vegetative, Animal, Speaking). Humans have the greatest Desire to Receive of any of creation, and they are described in this Kingdom as those who can speak. Humans are unique in that they can use the power of the spoken word to both create and destroy. See also: **Animal Kingdom, Inanimate Kingdom, Vegetative Kingdom**

*Ta'amei Torah* – The revealed wisdom of Kabbalah and the Torah. All secrets and teachings of Kabbalah and the Torah can be divided into two categories: *Sitrei Torah* and *Ta'amei Torah*. Literally "taste or meaning of the Torah," *Ta'amei Torah* refers to the teachings of the Torah where there is a clear and understandable explanation for each connection we make in our daily life through studying and performing the Precepts. These teachings are usually not concealed and are made known to everyone. See: **Concealed Torah**

*Tazria* **(Woman who Conceives)** – This is the fourth portion of the Book of Leviticus in the Torah and talks about the laws of purity for a woman who has recently given birth, together with the laws pertaining to leprosy and the leper.

*Teshuvah* **(Repentance)** – Meaning literally "to return," *Teshuvah* is the process of going back to an earlier phase where things were connected to the source. When we "short circuit" (i.e., make a wrong choice) and conduct ourselves with selfishness, we disconnect from the Light of the Creator and attract chaos. *Teshuvah* is designed to reverse our negative consciousness through positive transformation, thus allowing us to reconnect with the Light of the Creator. When we take responsibility and own up to our past mistakes, we preemptively remove whatever chaos and pain we might face in the future as a result of our negativity. See also: **Cleaving**

**Ten** *Sefirot* – The 10 Emanations or spiritual building blocks that form the structure of the unseen universe. Every spiritual entity is made up of these Ten *Sefirot*. The first *Sefira* (singular for *Sefirot*) is *Keter* (Crown), which is the seed for the following *Sefirot*. After *Keter* come the other nine *Sefirot*: *Chochmah* (Wisdom), *Binah* (Understanding), *Chesed* (Mercy), *Gevurah* (Judgment/ Might), *Tiferet* (Beauty), *Netzach* (Eternity/Victory), *Hod* (Glory), *Yesod* (Foundation), and *Malchut* (Kingdom). *Malchut* brings to fruition all the seeds that were planted in *Keter*. The *Ten Luminous Emanations* is the study of the Ten *Sefirot*.

**Tet Sefirot** – The upper nine levels of the Ten *Sefirot*, these nine *Sefirot* are constantly connected to the Light of the Creator. The tenth and lowest level *Sefira* is *Malchut*, which connects and disconnects at times to the Light; *Malchut* is the only level of the Ten *Sefirot* that includes chaos and darkness.

**This World** – The physical world that we live in, where we are subject to the laws of cause and effect, and bound by the limitations of time, space, and motion. Also called the 1 Percent Reality and the illusionary world.

**Tikkun (Correction)** –The process by which we correct, cleanse, and elevate our soul. We came to this world to "correct" the selfish aspects of our nature and to transform ourselves into beings of sharing. Thus, everything we experience in life—good or bad—is a *Tikkun*. The purpose of this process is to bring every human being, along with the entire universe, to perfection. The process is also known as karma and the purpose of reincarnation.

**Tikkunei haZohar** (*Corrections to the Zohar*) – This book addresses the same general subject matter as the *Zohar*, but it is written as 72 commentaries on *"Beresheet,"* the first word of the *Book of Genesis* (in Hebrew, *Beresheet*). *Tikkunei haZohar* discourses upon teachings specifically directed to the Age of Aquarius. This is the first learning that Rav Shimon bar Yochai received in the cave where he lived for years in hiding from the Romans.

**Tosefot** – Literally meaning "additions," the *Tosefot* is a compilation of commentaries on the *Gemarah* (*Talmud*) that were authored by more than 100 sages. Foremost among these sages was the grandson of *Rashi*, Rav Shmuel ben Meir, also known as the *Rashbam*, who wrote most of the commentaries, which take the form of critical and explanatory comments.

**Tractate** – The *Talmud* and *Mishnah* are each divided into six sections called orders, with each order being further divided into subsections called *masechet* or tractates. Each subsection or tractate is given a name that describes the topic under discussion.

**Tractate *Avot* (Fathers)** – Also known as *Pirkei Avot* (*Lessons of Our Fathers*), this is one of the very few tractates in the *Mishnah* that does not have a *Gemarah* commentary on it. This tractate consists of ethical and moral principles and wise sayings to live by.

**Tractate *Ketuvot* (Marriage contract)** – *Ketuvot* is the plural of *Ketuba*, a document in Jewish marriage that outlines the rights and responsibilities of a groom in relation to his bride. Tractate *Ketuvot* is the second tractate of the third order of the *Mishnah* and teaches the material and moral laws and obligations of a husband and wife to each other.

**Tractate *Niddah* (Menstruation)** – This tractate discusses the laws of *niddah* (menstruation) for both married and unmarried women. The main focus of the discussion is sexual matters and purity.

**Tractate *Sanhedrin* (Assembly)** – The fourth tractate of the fourth order of the *Mishnah*, this tractate deals mostly with the technicalities of criminal law within the Jewish community.

**Tractate *Shabbat*** – The first tractate of the second order of the *Mishnah*, this tractate teaches the laws of *Shabbat*, delineating the obligations and prohibitions one is advised to follow in order to connect best to the energy that is available on *Shabbat*.

**Tractate *Uktzin*** – The last tractate of the sixth order of the *Mishnah* (the order covering *Taharot* or Purities), this tractate discusses the laws pertaining to the impurity that is found in the stems or peels of fruits and vegetables. There is no *Gemarah* commentary on this tractate.

**Tractate *Yevamot* (Levirate Marriage)** – Tractate *Yevamot* is the first tractate of the third order of the *Mishnah* and teaches the laws of levirate marriage, where the law of the Torah obligates a man's brother to marry the man's widow if the man dies without children. *Yevamot* also teaches the laws pertaining to incest and abandoned wives as well.

***Tree of Life*** - See: ***Etz haChaim***

***Tzimtzum* (Contraction)** – The Vessel's voluntary rejection or restriction of the Divine Light from the Endless World due to the concept of Bread of Shame and the Vessel's desire to be independent and God-like. In the lower physical world, this restriction, if not done voluntarily, is imposed. Restriction constitutes one of the basic rules by which our mundane reality operates.

**Vegetative Kingdom** – Of the four Kingdoms (Inanimate, Vegetative, Animal, Speaking), this is the second level, with a more intense Desire to Receive than the Inanimate Kingdom, but less desire than the Animal and Speaking Kingdoms. See also: **Animal Kingdom, Inanimate Kingdom, Speaking Kingdom**

**Vessel** – Every created being, physical or spiritual, is called Vessel. It is an entity that was designed to reveal a certain Light. The spiritual "size" or *komah* of the Vessel determines the amount of Light that it is meant to reveal.

**Way of Repentance (Way of Torah)** – There are two ways to achieve a better connection to the Light of the Creator, as well as personal and global transformation. Both ways grant the same result. The Way of Repentance involves personal positive transformation and continuous spiritual growth. When we proactively change our nature and work on ourselves and our negative traits, we will cleanse our negativity away without any real pain and suffering. It is the easy way to connect with the Light, one where only our ego will get hurt, not our soul. See also: **Way of Suffering**

**Way of Suffering** – One of the two ways to achieve a better connection to the Light of the Creator, as well as personal and global transformation. Both ways grant the same result. The Way of Suffering is a cleansing process that is filled with chaos, pain, and suffering; it occurs when we refuse to acknowledge our negative behaviors and to proactively change our nature. If we do not change our nature on our own, the change will happen by force and it will be through physical suffering and pain, challenges, chaos, and emptiness. See also: **Way of Repentance**

**Wisdom of Truth** – Another term for the Wisdom of Kabbalah, so called because truth is something that is neither subjective nor inconsistent. Truth is a constant and does not change because of human influences.

**World of the Endless (*Ein Sof*)** – The first reality before the beginning of Creation. The name in Hebrew (*Ein Sof,* literally "without end") indicates that this World has no end and no limitation of any kind, so the Light of the Creator shines unendingly. The worlds that were created after the World of *Ein Sof* were limited by the capacity of their vessels to receive the Light.

**World of Action (*Asiyah*)** – The lowest (from above downwards) of the Five Spiritual Worlds that emerged after the *Tzimtzum* (Contraction) of the Vessel in the World of the Endless. The World of Action is the dimension where the least amount of Light is revealed. This enables human beings to exercise their free will in discerning between good and evil. This World is also related to the *Sefira* of *Malchut* (Kingdom) and is referred to as the Tree of Knowledge of Good and Evil. See also: **Worlds *(Olamot)***

**World of Creation (*Beriah*)** – The third (from above downwards) of the Five Spiritual Worlds that appeared after the *Tzimtzum*

(Contraction). This World is related to the *Sefira* of *Binah* (Intelligence) and is a universal energy store. *Beriah* is also related to the *Shechinah* and is almost completely protected from the *klipot* (shells). See also: *Klipot, Shechinah,* Worlds *(Olamot)*

World of Emanation *(Atzilut)* – The second (from above downwards) of the Five Spiritual Worlds that appeared after the *Tzimtzum* (Contraction). In this high and most exalted World, the Vessel is passive in relation to the Light, allowing the Light to flow without any agenda. This World is related to the *Sefira* of *Chochmah* (Wisdom) and is completely protected from the *klippot* (shells). See also: *Klippot,* Worlds *(Olamot)*

World of Formation *(Yetzirah)* – The fourth (from above downwards) of the Five Spiritual Worlds that appeared after the *Tzimtzum* (Contraction). Whereas in the lowest World (Action), evil is the predominant force, in the World of Formation, goodness is the predominant force. This World is related to the *Sefira* of *Zeir Anpin* (Small Face) and to the energy of the Shield of David. See also: Worlds *(Olamot)*

World to Come – A realm where only happiness, fulfillment, love, and joy exist. This is the 99 Percent Realm of the Light of the Creator. The kabbalists explain that the World to Come exists in each and every moment of our lives. Every action of ours creates an effect that comes back to us either for good and for bad. Through the way we live our lives, we can create worlds according to our design. The World to Come is commonly referred to as the reality of life-after-life.

Worlds *(Olamot)* – A term used in the *Study of the Ten Luminous Emanations* to refer to the Five Spiritual Worlds. There are five channels that bring the Light down to our mundane reality. When these channels are filled with Light, we call them Worlds. Each World represents a different level of consciousness that is related to a level of veil that covers the Light. The word *olam* in Hebrew means "disappearance," referring to the fact that only when the Light is concealed can a reality be revealed. The Five Spiritual Worlds, from highest to lowest, are: Primordial Man (*Adam Kadmon*), Emanation (*Atzilut*), Creation (*Beriah*), Formation (*Yetzirah*), and Action (*Asiyah*). See also: **Klipot**

**Zohar (Book of Splendor)** –The major book of Kabbalah. The *Zohar* was written by the great sage Rav Shimon bar Yochai, who lived in the 2nd century BCE. This 23-volume work is the basis and source of all the teachings of Kabbalah that we have today. According to the kabbalists, there are many benefits to be gained from reading the *Zohar* or even from simply scanning its words.

## About the Author

 Born in Poland in 1886, **Kabbalist Rav Yehuda Ashlag** is revered by students of Kabbalah as one of the most profound mystics and spiritual teachers of the 20th Century. Among his many accomplishments was the first-ever translation of the *Zohar* from its original Aramaic into Hebrew.

Rav Ashlag felt a powerful need to reveal the wisdom of Kabbalah to the masses, which had previously been prohibited. This desire led him to found The Kabbalah Centre in Jerusalem in 1922, making the wisdom widely available for the first time, and thus passing on a legacy that continues to this day through Kabbalah Centre International, its teachers and students worldwide. He was the teacher and spiritual master of Rav Yehuda Brandwein, to whom leadership of The Centre was passed when Rav Ashlag died in 1954. In turn, when Rav Brandwein died in 1969, he designated Kabbalist Rav Berg to lead The Centre.

# More Ways to Bring the Wisdom of Kabbalah into your Life

*The Wisdom of Truth: 12 Essays by the Holy Kabbalist Rav Yehuda Ashlag*
**Edited by Michael Berg**

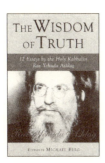

All of the essential truths of Kabbalah are encapsulated in these thought-provoking essays by arguably the most profound mystic of the 20th century. Originally published in 1984 as Kabbalah: A Gift of the Bible, and long out of print, this is a new translation from the Hebrew, edited and with an introduction by noted Kabbalah scholar Michael Berg.

*And You Shall Choose Life: An Essay on Kabbalah, The Purpose of Life, and Our True Spiritual Work*
**By Rav Ashlag, Edited by Michael Berg**

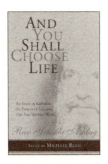

Preceding the time this essay was written in 1933-34, Kabbalah was considered taboo. But Rav Ashlag, the founder of The Kabbalah Centre, was a visionary pioneer. This book gives insight into one of the greatest kabbalistic thought leaders of all time. One of the most challenging aspects is the tone of urgency. As people were swept up in pain and suffering, Rav Ashlag tried to explain that despite outer events, the Creator is good. "Choosing life" means forming a connection to God, removing ego and pursuing the spiritual path of Kabbalah. Although written many decades ago, the essays are timeless.

### On World Peace
### By Rav Ashlag
### Edited by Michael Berg

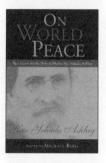

Everything that exists in reality, whether good or bad—including even the most evil and damage-causing thing in the world—has the right to exist, to the degree that destroying it and removing it completely from the world is forbidden. In these short but powerful treatises, Rav Ashlag explains that evil (or that which is not good), is nothing more than a work in progress and that upon arrival at our final destination *all things*, even the most damaged will be good. This remarkable perspective helps us to view with awe the system the Creator has given us to develop and grow, and to gain certainty in the end of the journey.

As the handwriting of a righteous person contains spiritual energy, *On World Peace* includes copies of Rav Ashlag's original writings. The book is nothing less than a gift to humanity.

### The Thought of Creation
### By Rav Ashlag
### Edited by Michael Berg

In *Thought of Creation*, Rav Ashlag describes the original thought of the Creator, which was to give humanity endless life full of joy and happiness, in a perfect universe, free of chaos, pain and suffering. He also wanted to give us the greatest gift of all—free will, something neither animals nor angels possess. In order to exercise free will and the blessings of sharing, independence, and the ability to create, He allowed us to leave his perfect world. This resulted in a temporary flawed physical universe in which we can work to bring it into perfection.

Each of us has a responsibility to help recreate this world, says Rav Ashlag, and by using the tools of Kabbalah and the *Zohar* we can bring it to perfection with peace, love, joy and fulfillment resounding in every corner of the universe.

### Beloved of My Soul: Letters from Rav Brandwein to Rav Berg
### Edited by Michael Berg

It is said the greatest love exists between a student and his spiritual teacher. In a bond of study, their hearts and consciousness are united. As these two souls on a path converge, they carry the lineage of previous masters, and ignite the way for future generations of students. This book is a rare glimpse into such a relationshipThrough the 37 letters presented here, written from Rav Brandwein to Rav Berg between 1965 and 1969, we gain deep insights into loving spiritual lessons from teacher to student. The letters are presented without a filter of interpretation, allowing readers to leave with answers—and more questions—and a yearning for greater wisdom. Rav Brandwein always instructed Rav Berg to review each letter at least three times and see what he could derive to help with his own service of God.

### Secrets of the Zohar: Stories and Meditations to Awaken the Heart
### By Michael Berg

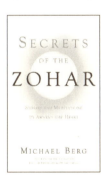

*The Zohar*'s secrets are the secrets of the Bible, passed on as oral tradition and then recorded as a sacred text that remained hidden for thousands of years. They have never been revealed quite as they are here in these pages, which decipher the codes behind the best stories of the ancient sages and offer a special meditation for each one. Entire portions of the *Zohar* are presented, with the Aramaic and its English translation in side-by-side columns. This allows you to scan and to read aloud so that you can draw on the *Zohar*'s full energy and achieve spiritual transformation. Open this book and open your heart to the Light of the *Zohar*!

# The *Zohar*

Composed more than 2,000 years ago, the 23-volume *Zohar* is a commentary on biblical and spiritual matters written in the form of conversations among teachers. It was given to all humankind by the Creator to bring us protection, to connect us with the Creator's Light, and ultimately to fulfill our birthright of transformation. The *Zohar* is an effective tool for achieving our purpose in life.

More than eighty years ago, when The Kabbalah Centre was founded, the *Zohar* had virtually disappeared from the world. Today, all this has changed. Through the editorial efforts of Michael Berg, the *Zohar* is available in the original Aramaic language and for the first time in English with commentary.

# We teach Kabbalah, not as a scholarly study but as a way of creating a better life and a better world.

## WHO WE ARE

The Kabbalah Centre is a non-profit organization that makes the principles of Kabbalah understandable and relevant to everyday life. The Kabbalah Centre teachers provide students with spiritual tools based on kabbalistic principles that students can then apply as they see fit to improve their own lives and by doing so, make the world better. The Centre was founded by Rav Yehuda Ashlag in 1922 and now spans the globe with brick-and-mortar locations in more than 40 cities as well as an extensive online presence. To learn more, visit www.kabbalah.com.

## WHAT WE TEACH

There are five core principles:

- **Sharing:** Sharing is the purpose of life and the only way to truly receive fulfillment. When individuals share, they connect to the force of energy that Kabbalah calls the Light—the Infinite Source of Goodness, the Divine Force, the Creator. By sharing, one can overcome ego—the force of negativity.

- **Awareness and Balance of the Ego:** The ego is a voice inside that directs people to be selfish, narrow-minded, limited, addicted, hurtful, irresponsible, negative, angry, and hateful. The ego is a main source of problems because it allows us to believe that others are separate from us. It is the opposite of sharing and humility. The ego also has a positive side, as it motivates one to take action. It is up to each individual to choose whether they act for themselves or whether to also act in the well-being of others. It is important to be aware of one's ego and to balance the positives and negatives.

- **Existence of Spiritual Laws:** There are spiritual laws in the universe that affect people's lives. One of these is the Law of Cause and Effect: What one puts out is what one get back, or what we sow is what we reap.

- **We Are All One:** Every human being has within him- or herself a spark of the Creator that binds each and every person into one totality. This understanding informs us of the spiritual precept that every human being must be treated with dignity at all times, under any circumstances. Individually, everyone is responsible for war and poverty in all parts of the world and individuals can't enjoy true and lasting fulfillment as long as others are suffering.

- **Leaving Our Comfort Zone Can Create Miracles:** Becoming uncomfortable for the sake of helping others taps us into a spiritual dimension that ultimately brings Light and positivity to our lives.


## HOW WE TEACH

**Courses and Classes.** On a daily basis, The Kabbalah Centre focuses on a variety of ways to help students learn the core kabbalistic principles. For example, The Centre develops courses, classes, online lectures, books, and audio products. Online courses and lectures are critical for students located around the world who want to study Kabbalah but don't have access to a Kabbalah Centre in their community. To learn more, visit www.ukabbalah.com.

**Spiritual Services and Events.** The Centre organizes and hosts a variety of weekly and monthly events and spiritual services where students can participate in lectures, meditation and share meals together. Some events are held through live streaming online. The Centre organizes spiritual retreats and tours to energy sites, which are places that have been closely touched by great kabbalists. For example, tours take place at locations where kabbalists may have studied or been buried, or where ancient texts like the *Zohar* were authored. International events provide students from all over the world with an opportunity to make connections to unique energy available at certain times of the year. At these events, students meet with other students, share experiences and build friendships.

**Volunteering.** In the spirit of Kabbalah's principles that emphasize sharing, The Centre provides a volunteer program so that students can participate in charitable initiatives, which includes sharing the wisdom of Kabbalah itself through a mentoring program. Every year, hundreds of student volunteers organize projects that benefit their communities such as feeding the homeless, cleaning beaches and visiting hospital patients.

**One-on-One.** The Kabbalah Centre seeks to ensure that each student is supported in his or her study. Teachers and mentors are part of the educational infrastructure that is available to students 24 hours a day, seven days a week.

Hundreds of teachers are available worldwide for students as well as a study program for their continued development. Study takes place in person, by phone, in study groups, through webinars, and even self-directed study in audio format or online. To learn more visit, www.ukabbalah.com.

**Publishing.** Each year, The Centre translates and publishes some of the most challenging kabbalistic texts for advanced scholars including the *Zohar*, *Writings of the Ari*, and the *Ten Luminous Emanations with Commentary*. Drawing from these sources The Kabbalah Centre publishes books yearly in more than 30 languages that are tailored for both beginner- and intermediate-level students and distributed around the world.

**Zohar Project.** The *Zohar*, the primary text of kabbalistic wisdom, is a commentary on biblical and spiritual matters composed and compiled over 2000 years ago and is believed to be a source of Light. Kabbalists believe that when it is brought into areas of darkness and turmoil, the *Zohar* can create change and bring about improvement. The Kabbalah Centre's *Zohar* Project shares the *Zohar* in 30 countries by distributing free copies to organizations and individuals in recognition of their service to the community and to areas where there is danger. Since 2007, over 400,000 copies of the *Zohar* were donated to hospitals, embassies, places of worship, universities, not-for-profit organizations, emergency services, war zones, natural disaster locations, soldiers, pilots, government officials, medical professionals, humanitarian aid workers, and more.

In appreciation of my father

Lazer ben Avraham

A man with a love of children;
who gives of himself freely,
and who always has a kind word.

His example is a blessing.

Daniel ben Lazer